DATE DUE

PRINTED IN U.S.A.

Planning and Financing the New Venture

JEFFRY A. TIMMONS

Babson College & Harvard Business School

Planning and Financing the New Venture

BRICK HOUSE PUBLISHING COMPANY
Acton, Massachusetts

Dedication

To the Price Institute for Entrepreneurial Studies,
and to my friends Harold Price and Gloria Appel
and the Trustees, for their dedicated and pioneering
support of entrepreneurship education.

Library of Congress Cataloging-in-Publication Data

Timmons, Jeffry A.
  Planning and financing the new venture / Jeffrey A.
  Timmons.
  p. cm.
  Includes bibliographical references.
  ISBN 0-931790-92-1 : ISBN 0-931790-93-X (pbk.)
  1. New business enterprises—Planning. 2. New business
  enterprises—Finance.   I. Title.
HD62 . 5 . T56   1990   89-22115
658 . 1 ' 1—dc20   CIP

Contents

Preface

There is a substantial body of knowledge that entrepreneurs need to acquire if they are to get the odds in their favor, including knowing how to develop a business plan, knowing where to raise capital and how to get it, knowing how to value and finance the venture, and knowing how to prepare for a harvest.

This book examines how successful entepreneurs approach resources and use other people's resources, by focusing on minimizing, controlling and using resources, rather than just on owning them. The book also examines the process of selecting and managing outside professsionals—accountants, lawyers, consultants, and board members.

Advice is given on why a business plan should be written, how to prepare for it, and how to construct the necessary various financial statements.

There are comprehensive discussions and summaries of all the sources of capital available to entrepreneurs, including debt and equity and private, venture and government sources.

Explored at length is how to obtain capital from venture capital firms, informal capital sources, banks and other commercial lenders. Also discussed are the valuation of the venture, the negotiation and structuring of the deal, and the investment agreement.

Finally, the book looks at why a harvest goal is important for entrepreneurs, the harvest options, how to craft a harvest strategy, and some of the issues beyond achieving a harvest, including the unavoidable reality: you can't take it with you.

The appendixes include a detailed business plan guide, usable as a tool for shaping a highly professional business plan, an outline of a venture capital investment agreement, a sample term sheet, and a sample stock restriction and vesting agreement.

Planning and Financing the New Venture is the third of three related books. *The Entrepreneurial Mind* was the first, and *New Business Opportunities* was the second. This book and its two companions are rooted in both real-world applications and nearly two decades of refinement in the classroom. They are direct descendants of my earlier book, *New Venture Creation*, which has been become a leading textbook for courses in entrepreneurship and starting new ventures worldwide, and according to the *Wall Street Journal* (October 1987), a "textbook classic."

These books have two principal roots, going back over twenty years. Since 1971, and earlier doing doctoral research at the Harvard Business School, I have been immersed in the world of entrepreneurs and the start-up, development, financing and harvesting of new and growing (and sometimes shrinking) companies: as a student, researcher, teacher and scholar, and as an investor, advisor, director and founding shareholder.

The content and material of these books have won accolades from experienced MBAs, college seniors and hundreds of founders and owners of new and emerging companies pursuing their entrepreneurial dreams. Much of what is here is has been tempered and enhanced by my working directly with these entrepreneurs and entrepreneural firms—and usually while risking both my reputation and my wallet.

The Entrepreneurial Mind addresses what makes entrepreneurs tick and what they do—and avoid—to get the odds of success in their favor. How do they convert their dreams to tangible visions and to commercial realities? What do successful entrepreneurs do differently that enables them not only to survive but to "grow up big"? How do these entrepreneurs think and act? What are their winning strategies and approaches? How do they do their homework? What do they pay a lot of attention to—and know they can ignore?

The answers too these questions unlock part of the mystery of entrepreneurship. Once you know how winning entrepreneurs think, act and perform, then you can establish goals to practice emulating those actions, attitudes, habits and strategies. Certainly, the book does not pretend to know how to "make silk purses out of sows ears," but it has received quite favorable comments from numerous world-class entrepreneurs, including:

Peter J. Sprague, Chairman, National Semiconductor Corporation: "Your book is a revelation. You could have saved me a great deal of trouble and money if you had written it twenty years ago!"

J. W. Marriott, Jr., Chairman & President, Marriott Corporation: "Truly outstanding! Congratulations to you on your fine contribution to the society of entrepreneurs."

Royal Little, Late Founder and Chairman, Textron Corporation and Narragansett Capital: "I was tremendously impressed with the thoroughness with which you covered this complicated subject."

New Business Opportunities is aimed at "getting you to the right place at the right time." With 20-20 hindsight, and oversimplification, most people think it is just a matter of coincidence. Savvy, successful entrepreneurs (even if they have not read *The Entrepreneurial Mind*!) know it isn't nearly so easy. They know that a good opportunity is more than just a good idea. Judging by small-firm failure statistics—as many as 9 out of 10 new firms fail in ten years—most of these "good ideas" do not work out. What may surprise you, even big companies do not fare any better: only about 1 in 10 of the new products brought to the shelves of America's supermarkets survive more than one year. And this is usually after months and millions of dollars spent on market research and testing.

What is a good opportunity? Why and how do successful entrepreneurs often find the best opportunities? How can you find or create such opportunities? Would you recognize one when you see it? Do you know what to say 'no' to? What are the things to look for and look out for, in order to get the odds of success and the reward-risk balance in your favor? The answers to these and other questions will help you to think big and avoid wild-goose chases.

Judging by some early feedback from some of America's top entrepreneurs, *New Business Opportunities* is on the right track:

"*New Business Opportunities* is right on target—focusing on execution as opposed to just having the ideas. I can heartily endorse this book." Nolan K. Bushnell, Chairman, Axlon, and founder, Atari Corporation.

"As practical as it is logical. *New Business Opportunities* is a bible for the entrepreneur." Roger A. Enrico, President and Chief Executive Officer, Pepsi-Cola Company.

"This book is long overdue! *New Business Opportunities* lays to rest the myth that all you need is a good idea to succeed in business. Once you have an idea, you need to execute it. Jeff Timmons tells us how." Charles M. Leighton, Chairman, CML Group.

"The book combines a real handbook with a road atlas to entrepreneurial success in a single volume. It sits within one arm's length of my desk. Sincere congratulations." Stanley Rich, founder and CEO, Venture Resource Associates, and co-founder and past chairman, MIT Enterprise Forum.

"Timmons takes the mystery and magic out of that foreign word, 'entrepreneur,' and directs us to reality, to the living, working world. As he does this he magnifies that word with meaning and gives useful direction." Trammell Crow, Trammell Crow Company.

"Your book reminds us that running a business in today's world is to be deeply aware of market trends, the barriers to new entry, capital requirements, the need for expanding new products, and managing the unpredictable business environment." M. Gilbert Trigano, Chairman and CEO, Club Med.

"I greatly enjoyed reading your book. *New Business Opportunities* is a reference book for all entrepreneurs and should be on every entrepreneurial team's desk." Bert W. M. Twaalfhoven, International Entrepreneur, Industrialist and Venture Capitalist.

Jeffry A. Timmons
Harvard, Massachusetts
September 1989

About the Author

Jeffry A. Timmons is nationally and internationally known for his work in new ventures, venture capital, venture financing and entrepreneurship. He is currently the first holder of both the Frederic C. Hamilton Professorship at Babson College and the Class of 1954 Professorship at the Harvard Business School. He joined Babson in 1982, as Paul T. Babson Professor, and has served as Director of the Center for Entrepreneurial Studies and the Price-Babson College Fellows Program. He has developed and teaches courses on starting new ventures and financing entrepreneurial ventures, and the Entrepreneurial Management Program for the presidents and executives of emerging businesses.

In 1971 he became a founding shareholder of Venture Founders Corporation, a Boston venture capital firm with subsidiaries in the U.K. and Belgium, with over $65 million under management. He worked closely with VFC from 1971–82 in developing ways to identify, evaluate and finance seed-stage and stage-up ventures.

Through his own firm, Curtis-Palmer & Company, Inc., founded in 1981, his clientele has included presidents and partners of venture capital firms and emerging companies in the U.S., U.K. and Sweden, including Investkontakt & Svetab, Venture Founders Corporation, Zero Stage Capital, Venture Economics (publisher of *Venture Capital Journal*), Vlasic Foods (part of Campbell Soup) and The Sunmark Companies, a $160M+ private firm in St. Louis recently acquired by Nestle.

In 1981–82 he accepted a full-time assignment in Stockholm with one of the first venture capital firms there.

In 1984, as the first outside member of of the partnership committee of Cellular One in Boston, he became actively involved in starting and building the first independent car phone company in New England. In 1987 he became a founding shareholder and director of Boston Communications Group (BCG), which owns and operates cellular phone systems in southern Maine and New Hampshire, cellular phone installation and service centers, a cellular-credit card phone company and other telecommunications ventures.

Since 1985 he has assisted Ernst & Young's national Entrepreneurial Services Group to develop and implement professional development programs for partners in this leading Big Eight accounting firm, including Emerging Businesses & Entrepreneurship, and Financing Alternatives. This effort is now expanding to E&Y International in a similar effort for Canada and the United Kingdom.

In 1988 he joined the Advisory Board of Bridge Capital Investors, a $150 million bridge fund in Teaneck, New Jersey, which specializes in providing growth capital for emerging companies with sales in the $5–100 million range.

Of particular note is that these investing activities have spanned a range of high, low, and no technology businesses, and product and service businesses in the U.S., Canada, U.K. and Europe.

In addition to the practical experience noted above, Professor Timmons has conducted research in entrepreneurship on new and emerging firms and venture financing, which has resulted in nearly one hundred papers and articles in such publications as *Harvard Business Review* and *Journal of Business Venturing*, and in the proceedings of national and international conferences, including *Frontiers of Entrepreneurship Research* (1981–89). He is also quoted in publications such as *Wall Street Journal, INC., Working Woman, Success, Money, Venture, Business Week, Entrepreneur, In Business, The Chicago Tribune, The New York Times, The Boston Globe, Los Angeles Times*, and elsewhere.

He has authored and co-authored several books, including *The Entrepreneurial Mind* and *New Business Opportunities* (Brick House, 1989), *New Venture Creation* (Richard D. Irwin, 1985), *The Encyclopedia of Small Business Resources* (Harper & Row, 1984), *The Insider's Guide to Small Business Resources* (Doubleday, 1982), *A Region's Struggling Savior* (SBA, 1980), and has co-edited three years of *Frontiers in Entrepreneurship Research* (Babson College, 1983, 1984 and 1985). His speaking and consulting assignments have included travels throughout the U.S. and Austria, Australia, Canada, Philippines, U.K., Scandanavia, Spain and elsewhere.

He is a graduate of Colgate University and received his MBA and doctorate from Harvard Business School.

Acknowledgements

There are many contributors to the ideas behind this book from whom I have drawn intellectual capital, and have received support and encouragement as well as inspiration. To list them all might well comprise a chapter by itself. Short of that, I wish to express special thanks to those who have been so helpful in recent years. First, my colleagues at Babson College and Harvard Business School who have been a constant source of encouragement, inspiration and friendship: Bill Bygrave, Alan Cohen, Neil Churchill, Jeff Ellis, Ned Goodhue, Dan Muzyka, Bob Reiser, Natalie Taylor, Bill Wetzel, Mel Copen, Bill Dill, J. B. Kassarjian, Tom Moore, and Gordon Prichett. Then our Price-Babson College Fellows: Stan Rich, Chuck Schmidt, Randy Wise, and especially Les Charm for his generous giving of time, entrepreneurial energy and resources to Babson. And all of the inductees into Babson's Academy of Distinguished Entrepreneurs, who have shared their entrepreneurial lives with us and have contributed so much to the legend and legacy of entrepreneurship at Babson College.

My dear friend and colleague, Professor Howard H. Stevenson, first Sarofim-Rock Professor at the Harvard Business School, stands alone for his support and generous sharing of his "world-class" intellectual capital and extraordinary wit. Howard, more than anyone else, has caused the academic community to focus on the role of opportunity in the entrepreneurial process.

Others who have been instrumental in furthering the entrepreneurial management mission and who have been supportive include Ron Fox, Bill Fruhan, Rosabeth Moss Kanter (first Class of 1960 Professor), Paul Lawrence, Marty Marshall, Dean John McArthur, Tom Piper, Mike Roberts, Bill Sahlman, and the Class of 1954.

Outside Babson and Harvard, several key people have given more to this effort than they shall ever know. Paul J. Tobin, president of Cellular

One, Boston and the Boston Communications Group, has been a model entrepreneur and entrepreneurial manager in pioneering the car phone industry in America, along with the superb team at Cell One (Bob, Jean and Kim). I learn new lessons on entrepreneurial creativity and the nose for an opportunity each time I work with P. J. and see him and the team in action.

A special thanks is due Alexander L. M. Dingee, Jr., founder and president of Venture Founders Corporation, Lexington, Massachusetts, for his contributions to much of the material on business planning and to the Business Plan Guide. His original work has been revised and additions made to it, but numerous real-life examples and many of the lessons are derived from his experience as an entrepreneur.

Several other entrepreneurs and venture capitalists have been both sources of encouragement and my educators: Brion Applegate, Gordon Baty, Karl Baumgartner, Bill Egan, Joe Frye, Dave Gumpert, Doug Kahn, Paul Kelley, Earl Linehan, Jack Peterson, Len Smollen, John Van Slyke and The Fabb. A special thanks to my colleagues at Bridge Capital: Don Remey, Bart Goodwin, Hoyt Goodrich, Bill Spencer and Geoff Wadsworth, and advisors Craig Foley, Bill Foxley and Dick Johnson.

Harold Price, founder and benefactor, and Gloria Appel and the late Edwin M. Appel, of the Price Institute, have been staunch and unwavering champions of entrepreneurship at Babson College and across America. Their generous, pioneering support of the Price-Babson Fellows Program has made a major contribution toward cloning entrepreneurial minds—in both faculty and students—at colleges and universities worldwide. They have exceeded their prevoiously extraordinary generosity by making a $500 million challenge grant to Babson's Center for Entrepreneurial Studies to help us continue the mission and our work.

Hal Seigle, retired Chairman of The Sunmark Companies, St. Louis, and now a professional director and advisor to growing companies, has taught me a great deal about the difference between working hard and working smart, and in appreciating the difference between an idea and an opportunity. Watching him do both, always with a lot of class and integrity, has been a post-graduate course by itself.

My colleagues at Ernst & Young's national office in the Entrepreneurial Services Group have opened my eyes to a whole new perspective of how it is possible for a Big Eight firm to be very entrepreneurial in seeking out new business opportunities and building their own business. They include: In the U. S., Tom Barton, Herb Braun, Gary Dando, Bill Casey, and Bruce Mantia (all in Cleveland), partners Ron Diegelman (Baltimore), Gayle Goodman (San Francisco), Rick Fox (Seattle), Dick Haddrill (Atlanta), Carl Mayhall (Dallas), Dick Nigon (Minneapolis), Ralph Sabin (Newport Beach), and Dale Sander (San Diego). In Canada, Jim Harper, Howard Crofts, Don Brown and Dan MacLean, all of Thorne, Ernst & Whinney. In the U. K., David Wilson, Will Rainey, David Wilkinson, Richard Harrison, Chris Harrison, Alan Clarke and Peter Gillett. They and Hy Shweil (Stamford) and members of the ESG Task Force have all worked with me to build a culture, a strategy and the know-how for providing value-added service opportunities as General Business Advisors to privately owned and emerging businesses.

A great debt of appreciation is perpetually due to all my former students from whom I learn with each encounter, and marvel both at their accomplishments and how little damage I imparted! Especially, Peter Altman, Avrum Belzar, Jeff Brown, Everett Dowling, Brian Dwyer, Joe Harris, Carl Hedberg, Greg Hunter, Jody Kosinski, Frank Mosvold, Greg Murphy, Steve Orne, Gerry Peterson, Steve Richards, Jim Turner and Marc Wallace, to name a few.

Finally, a special thanks is due Robert Runck, president of Brick House Publishing, whose unique entrepreneurial nose for opportunity was instrumental in making these three books possible. His creative approach to publishing ventures, and his excellent editorial wisdom and talent, is evident throughout the three books in this series. Without his energy, effort and contributions the books would never have been written. He is also living proof why smaller, entrepreneurial publishers can succeed in the land of the giants.

Introduction

We are in the midst of what I call the "The Silent Revolution," an unusual revolution of the human spirit and the marketplace: a discovery of the *extraordinary power of the entrepreneurial process.* By creating or recognizing and seizing opportunities, by providing imagination, tenacity and leadership, and by insisting on the higher ground of ethical and square dealing, successful entrepreneurs play for the long haul. In this complicated process they create and allocate value and benefits for individuals, groups, organizations and society.

The entrepreneurial roots and backbones of economic progress are now being discovered worldwide, and show unprecedented promise of a sustained, global entreprenuerial wave, including China and other eastern bloc nations. Lighting the flame of the entrepreneurial spirit empowers nations and peoples with "the knowledge and ability to fish, rather than just giving them a fish."

Among the adult working population in the U.S. about one in eight is self-employed, and it can be said that a cultural imperative exists in the minds of millions of other Americans: the entrepreneurial dream of working for oneself, of "growing up big." And it is no wonder, once you discover how self-employed feel about themselves and their work lives, and what the the economic rewards are. Uniformly, these self-employed persons report the highest levels of personal satisfaction, challenge, pride and remuneration. As a lot they love their work because it is invigorating, energizing and meaingful. Compared to managers and those working for others, as many as three times more never plan to retire. They seem to love the "entrepreneurial game" for the game's sake. The vast majority of the two million "millionaires" in the U.S. in 1987 have accumulated their wealth through entrepreneurial acts of self-employment.

What may be more surprising is that even graduates of the Harvard Business School—long thought of as the "West Point for the Fortune 500"—thrive on this entrepreneurial dream: about one-third end up working for themselves, and the vast majority of all graduates ten years after graduation work for companies employing fewer than one thousand people. Further evidence of just how wide and deep is the quest for entrepreneurship is reflected by the readership of the Harvard Business Review: about 70% are owners, executives or managers of firms with fewer than one thousand employees. And among the students at HBS, nearly 90% say they have the entrepreneurial dream of self-emplopment. A recent survey of Fortune 500 CEOs showed two dominant activities they considered the most prestigious: first, owning or investing in a small company, and second, international travel. One has to ask: what is going on here?

The rebirth of the "entrepreneurial wave" in America in the past decade has brought unprecedented benefits not just to individuals but to society as a whole. Entrepreneurs, it turns out, are the fuel, engine and throttle for the economic backbone of the country. Consider the following:

• About 1.3 million new enterprises from one-person operations and up will be launched in the U.S. in 1989. Contrast this with perhaps 200,000 a year 25 years ago, and 600,000 a year as recently as 1983.

• Entrepreneurship is not just the domain of new and small firms. It can also happen in old and large companies (though we see it far less frequently), in slower growing and even troubled companies, in profit-seeking and non-profit organizations, and in the eastern, western and developing economies. But what may be most singnificant of all: it also can *fail to occur.*

• Today there are about 19 million enterprises of all kinds in the U.S., and it is estimated that there will be 30 million by the year 2000. By 1985 there were nearly four million enterprises owned by women in the U.S., and between 1980 and 1985 the rate at which women were creating businesses was two to five times greater than all others. By the year 2000 40% or more of all businesses will be owned by one or more women, dramatic evidence of "the silent revolution. "

• The U.S. has the *same number* of people working in manufacturing jobs today as we did in 1966. Yet, since 1966 the nation's economy has added 30 million new jobs! What is more, virtually all of the net new jobs created in this country come from new and expanding firms—not from the large, established companies. One recent study reported than just 7% of these new and expanding ventures accounted for a remarkable 118% of all the net new jobs in the early 1980s. In 1987 employment in seven million small firms grew three times faster than employment in the 500 largest companies in the nation, according to American Express.

• Since World War II, half of all innovations and 95% of all radical innovations have come from new and smaller firms. Innumerable innovations and industries began this way: the heart pacemaker, the microcomputer, overnight express packages, the quick oil change, fast food, the oral contraceptive, the x-ray machine, and hundreds of others.

• Just 37 individual entrepreneurs inducted into the Babson College Academy of Distinguished Entrepreneurs in 1977–88 have created and/or built companies—many from nothing—to combined sales which would place their thirty-seven companies as the *20th largest GNP* in the world. Their names are entrepreneurial legends: Royal Little, An Wang, Frank Perdue, Ken Olsen, Sochio Honda, Ray Kroc, Fred Smith, Nolan Bushnell, Trammel Crow, Willard Marriott, Ed Lowe, Wally Amos, H. R. Block, Don Burr, John Cullinane, Rupert Murdoch, Peter Sprague, John Templeton, and others with equal deeds but lesser familiarity.

• The entrepreneurial fever has also spread to colleges and high schools in recent years, and now shows promise of gaining the attention of administrators and teachers in elementary schools. Over 400 colleges and universities offer courses in new ventures and entrepreneurship, compared to as few as 50 in 1975.

• Between $50 and $60 billion of informal risk capital exists in our economy, almost entirely coming from self-made entrepreneurs called "angels."

• Another $30 billion of venture capital funds are available from professional sources seeking to back small company entrepreneurs with big ambitions—Apple Computer, Federal Express, Lotus Software, Digital Equipment Corporation, Data General, and the like started with just such sources. Such funds are now a worldwide phenomenon, including the United Kingdom, Scandanavia, Western Europe, Spain, Kenya, Brazil, Australia, Philippines, Japan, Korea and others.

• For the first time ever, in June and July, 1987, 46 senior policy makers, researchers, entrepreneurs and executives from 26 countries met at the Salzburg Seminar in Austria for an eight-day session entitled "Entrepreneurship," led by Professor Howard H. Stevenson of Harvard. Only three Americans attended. The rest looked like a United Nations contingent: China, Russia, Romania, Turkey, Norway, West Germany, Poland, Scotland, Ireland, England, Egypt, Greece, Yugoslavia, Spain, Portugal, Sweden, Netherlands, Belguim, Austria, Malaysia, Singapore and others.

Planning and Financing the New Venture

1

Why Write a Business Plan?

You are enthusiastic about an idea for a new business. You think it has excellent market prospects and fits well with your skills, experience, personal values, and aspirations. What is your entry strategy, and your tangible vision for growth so as to create value? How can the business be harvested for a gain? What are the most significant risks and problems involved in launching the enterprise? What are its long-term profit prospects? What are its future financing and cash flow requirements? What will be the demands of operating lead times, seasonality, and facility location? What is your marketing and pricing strategy? What are the *minimal* resources needed, and how can you have access to and control them, rather than own them? Can you articulate the answers to these questions, show the evidence for your conclusions—and *put them in writing?*

The business plan is a written document that articulates what the opportunity conditions are, why the opportunity exists, the entry and growth strategy to seize it, and why you and your team have what it takes to execute the plan. It can also serve as the blueprint you will need actually to launch and build your business.

If you plan to seek venture capital, a business plan is a must. But it is more than a financing device. It is invaluable in defining and anticipating the potential risks, problems, and trade-offs of a venture. Also, by involving your prospective management team in the preparation of the plan, you can evaluate potential partners and gain their commitment. And the business plan plays a key role in making a venture grow and become profitable.

If you have never started a business before, a business plan is an excellent way to help evaluate and guide the start-up. Think of it as a tool to get the odds on your side. And, if you have not raised outside capital previously, a business plan is essential for attracting investor attention, or convincing a bank or other lender that you know what you are doing.

In replying to a student who asked, "Do we really have to prepare business plans?," Nolan Bushnell, founder of Atari and other ventures, had this to say: "That's exactly what you have to do. There is no way around it, you're doing the best thing. Every time you prepare a business plan you become a better entrepreneur—I really believe that."

Or take these comments from two would-be entrepreneurs:

Another lesson is the importance of doing a business plan. It may be pain in the neck, but it sure does pay off. If I had gone into the venture of importing copperware from France that I was thinking of without going through a detailed analysis of what had to be done to succeed in the business, and without seeing what the market really boiled down to in numbers, I would have fallen flat on my face, probably at a considerable financial loss. My feelings toward the venture were drastically different after the opportunity analysis and business plan than before.

One of the most important things I have learned is the importance of the business plan. Very successful entrepreneurs talk about how important it is. I wish I had known this before my brother-in-law and I started a microcomputer dealership. We really had no idea of what a business plan was. Looking back on it, I realize how awful our presentation to the investors was. We were lucky that most of them were close friends and families, and they knew us well. Otherwise, we never would have been able to raise all the capital we needed. Even though we were able to raise enough capital to start operations, the next time I start a business I will make sure I have a complete business plan.

For What and For Whom is a Business Plan?

The business plan has three principal uses: to raise money, to attract key management and other advisors, and to develop strategies and guidelines for growing the company. The most common purpose is for fund raising, including but not limited to venture capital, bank loans, leases, private placements with individual investors, strategic alliances with other firms, leveraged buyouts (LBOs), management buyouts (MBOs), acquisitions, expansion and harvesting the company.

Strategy development is an integral part of the process, whether it is for a start-up, an expansion, an acquisition, or to provide a locus for an operating plan and management discipline.

A well-developed business plan can also be a powerful tool for persuading key people to join you in your vision and quest. These can include—besides key management people—directors, vendors, customers and other critical outside resources. The best people are a very scarce commodity, so the more compelling your case, the higher the quality of people you will be able to attract.

The Rewards of Preparation

The development of a business plan for a start-up is neither quick nor easy. Properly preparing a plan may take two hundred hours or more. Squeezing that amount of time into evenings and weekends can make the process stretch out for months. Is such a time-consuming effort really worth the trouble? Wouldn't a more effective approach be to have an outside professional prepare the business plan, and then have the founders use their time to obtain financing and start the business?

No. The careful preparation of a business plan represents a unique opportunity to think through all the facets of a new venture. You can examine the consequences of different strategies and tactics and determine the human and financial requirements for launching and building the venture, all at no risk and little cost.

One entrepreneur discovered while preparing a business plan that the major market for his biomedical product was in nursing homes rather than in hospital emergency rooms, as he and his physician partner had previously assumed. This realization changed the focus of his entire marketing effort—before it was too late. Had he left the preparation to an outsider, it is unlikely he would have had the same sense of confidence and commitment to the new strategy.

Why Time is of the Essence: A Shortcut Plan

Sometimes events surrounding an opportunity are simply moving faster than you expected. You face a painful paradox: take the time to prepare a complete business plan and someone else seizes the market opportunity before you do; move ahead without a plan and end up paying a dumb price, or discovering risks and liabilities when it is too late to back out, or simply making an ill-informed decision to go ahead. Consider the following actual instance:

In 1986 I was one of a group of investors who discovered that MetroMedia Telecommunications had decided to sell their Cellular One car-phone business in Boston. Working with the existing management team, we decided to pursue the funding for a premptive bid before the property became "officially" for sale less than a month later. We estimated that we had two to four weeks to prepare a business plan, meet prospective investors and propose a deal to MetroMedia. Clearly, there was not enough time to develop a complete business plan. The "opportunity train" was flying along the track. What to do?

What we did was develop a "Mini Business Plan" or "Executive Summary Business Plan." It consisted of a dozen pages of key points, bulleted to highlight the significant issues covered by the business outline and executive summary described in the appendixes to this book (i.e., summary description of the business, market opportunity and entry strategy, target market size, growth and sales projections, competitive advantages, economics, profitability and harvest potential, the team and the proposed financing), with special emphasis on

• The management team and its outstanding performance in launching and building Cellular One in Boston.

• Market potential and penetration, and why the marketing strategy was working so well.

• The accounting systems and control software that had been developed and that was a leader in the industry.

• The critical assumptions behind the estimates of revenues and expenses.

• Summary financial statements, especially profit and loss, balance sheet and cash flow, with detailed backup.

All this was put together in just two to three days, and in three weeks commitments for more than $150 million were secured.

Such a plan can be used to feel out possible sources of funding. A three to eight page document highlighting the key points in the Executive Summary can also include names of key advisors, directors or backers.

A Plan's Long-term Value

Most founders find the business plan to be even more helpful after start-up. As the founder-president of one venture that grew to sales of $14 million in seven years put it:

Once you are in business, you realize that everyone, including the founders, is learning the job. If you have a thoughtful and complete business plan, you have a lot more confidence in your decisions. You have a reference already there to say, "Well, I have already run the numbers on inventory, or cost of goods, and this is what will happen."

The business plan can be especially valuable in the important area of product pricing. For instance:

The initial strategy of the founders of one new venture was to set the prices of its products below those of the competition, even though the venture had a superior product innovation in a growing market. When the founders consulted outside experts, they were persuaded to price 10% higher than the competition.

By its second year, the new company enjoyed pretax profits of $850,000 based on about $9 million in sales. The revised pricing strategy made a significant difference. Without the detailed analysis of the industry and competition that is central to the marketing section of the business plan, it is unlikely that outsiders would have seen the basis for a different pricing strategy.

Feedback on your business plan by trusted and knowledgeable outsiders can help in refining strategy and making difficult decisions:

A Nova Scotia entrepreneur who builds commercial fishing boats recently decided to raise his prices more than 40%, based on an outside analysis and critique of his business plan. He knew he would lose two orders, but he also knew he would make more profit on the remaining three than all five at the old price. His delivery time would be cut in half as well. He's convinced that the shortened delivery time will lead to additional sales at the higher margins. And with upfront and interim payments, he won't have to raise outside equity capital.

The process can also clarify the venture's financial requirements:

An entrepreneur with a three-year-old $1-million business erecting coal-loading sites believed he needed about $350,000 in expansion capital. After reflecting on a detailed critique of his business-plan presentation, he concluded, "The worst *thing I could do right now is put more money into the business. The first thing I should do is get my own backyard in order. But I will be back in two or three years."*

True to his prediction, he returned two-and-a-half years later. His company was now approaching $3 million in sales and had a business plan for expansion that resulted in a $400,000 debt capital investment, without relinquishing any ownership.

Planning from the Investor's Point of View

Once you have convinced yourself and your partners that your venture is viable on paper, can you also convince prospective investors? If you seek investment capital or loans, you will face skepticism from venture capital firms, banks, insurance companies, and other financing sources. For example, only 1% to 5% of proposals submitted to venture capital sources for start-up or on-going financing are actually funded.

An effective business plan will convince the investor that you have identified a high-growth opportunity with high profit potential, that you have the entrepreneurial and management talent to effectively exploit that opportunity, and that you have a rational, coherent and believable program for doing so. In essence, it conveys your understanding of why an opportunity exists, why you have an "unfair advantage" to exploit it, and the hurdles and wickets that must be navigated in order to succeed.

(A companion book to this one, *New Business Opportunities* [Brick House, 1989], provides a complete discussion of various screening criteria.)

For the investor, the business plan is the single most important screening device. Once the plan has passed initial screening, the investor may request the entrepreneur to make an oral presentation describing key features of the venture. If the investor is still interested, the plan will be given a more detailed evaluation and will become a prime measure of the founders' ability to define and analyze opportunities and problems and to identify and plan actions to deal with them.

Because of the great importance investors and lenders attach to the quality of the entrepreneurs *and* their complete understanding of the business they are preparing to enter, it is essential that you write the plan yourself. The investor wants to be sure that what he or she sees is what he or she's got—your own analysis and understanding of the venture opportunity and your commitment to it. Nothing less will do.

Common Misconceptions about Planning

Entrepreneurs tend to downgrade the writing of a business plan because of certain false notions they hold about it. Technical and scientific entrepreneurs share one misconception that I call the "better mousetrap fallacy." They frequently place unwarranted faith in a product or invention, especially if it is patented. Indeed, technological ideas must be sound, but marketability and marketing know-how generally outweigh technical elegance in the success equation. One new venture reached nearly $40 million in sales, yet has no patents on its products.

A second misconception new entrepreneurs often have is that the business plan is essentially a negotiating and selling tool for raising money. It isn't considered relevant or useful beyond that. Indeed, I have heard more than one entrepreneur comment that the plan is "destined for the circular file" once the funds are in the bank.

Such a view is dangerous for several reasons. To prospective partners, investors or suppliers, it communicates a shallow understanding of the requirements for creating a successful business. It can also signal a hustle—a search for fast money and hope for an early sellout—that creates mistrust of the entrepreneur. If the plan isn't a serious promise of what the team can deliver, should investors believe anything the founders assert? Besides, even if you raise money but cannot deliver on the sales and profits you claimed in the plan, then you will quite likely give up both more ownership and control of the business, and risk your credibility.

A third misconception some entrepreneurs have is a belief that the primary and most important task in the start-up process is to determine if they can raise money as proof that their idea is sound. This "cart before the horse" approach usually results in a hastily prepared business plan and exuberant shopping among prospective investors.

One team of three entrepreneurs quit their jobs and invested about $150,000—virtually their life savings—in an effort to raise money for their start-up *company. Eight months later they had almost forty rejections from venture capitalists and smaller investment bankers. They nearly had to abandon the business, with total losses, before being redirected at the eleventh hour to more receptive sources. Today, three years later, the company is doing over $10 million in sales.*

Because most venture capital firms are quite small—often no more than two or three partners—they generally cannot take the time needed to get to know each entrepreneur and to explain the details for rejection. They use the business plan for initial screening as well as for making investment decisions. I have met many entrepreneurs who, as long as two years later, still do not understand that they were unable to raise capital because their business plans were deficient.

A fourth misconception is a belief among some entrepreneurs that their particular plan has no fatal flaws. These entrepreneurs ignore the need to test the plan's soundness with knowledgeable outside sources. Entrepreneurs must first search for flaws in the market analysis—this would make further consideration of the venture unnecessary. Another potential flaw is excessive dependence on outside suppliers for important state-of-the-art components that materially affect product development and prices:

Viatron, a computer-leasing company that obtained substantial public and private financing in the late 1960s, was driven driven into bankruptcy in large part because its suppliers were unable to produce several semiconductors at low enough prices to enable Viatron to meet its own heavily promoted low prices.

More recently, Air Florida succumbed to bankruptcy, but for a different fatal reason. They had the venture capital, the airplanes, the crews and staff, the schedules, the airports and the travel agencies to handle their flights. What they failed to line up far enough in advance were the gate space commitments necessary to load and unload passengers.

A final misconception among some start-up and early-stage entrepreneurs seeking venture capital is the belief that retaining a minimum 51% control of the company is essential. This view seems to assume that control depends on the legal percentage of ownership rather than on management skill. In short, 51% of nothing is nothing. Compare this with the 20% ownership retained by the four founders of Digital Equipment Corporation. Today those holdings are valued in the billions of dollars.

Sound investment partners do not want to run your company—they invest in you and your team. More than anything else in the early going, the founders' actions are the ultimate controlling influence on the venture.

A "Harvesting" Tool

Among existing firms not backed by venture capital, the "harvest" issue is especially troublesome. Without a venture-capital backer, the prime motivator and driving force to realize a harvest—along with the skills, know-how and networks to make it happen—is absent from the deal. A business plan for an on-going business can significantly enhance its harvest potential and selling price. Such a document can focus on articulating why there is a major opportunity for a prospective buyer, much as a start-up business plan does for venture capital investors.

Finally, a business plan is used within existing firms to focus on an internal venture opportunity. Take for instance, one of the founders of a firm that has grown to $20 million in sales in about a dozen years. He used a business plan to present to his board and partners an articulate statement of an opportunity for internal expansion—a new business from within.

Business Planning—Not for Everyone ... But

How can you determine an effective planning process for your venture? After all, business planning is not for everyone. There are times when it is more important to "do" than to plan. For instance, when an opportunity that makes sense for you to seize is perishing at a faster rate than you can complete a business plan articulating it, you are better off simply to act.

When you do write a plan, a thorough knowledge of yourself and your business is the place to begin, according to Phillip Thurston. He warns against the excesses of "planning systems" which have emerged in recent years. Nonetheless, he observes that:

The smaller companies weathering the current difficult economic times seem to be those following an idea—call it a no-frills, down-to-earth, but clear plan—of how to take advantage of the environment and how to allocate resources.[1]

Aside from the obvious need for a business plan for those entrepreneurs seeking to raise venture capital, what other dimensions, unique to you and your business, might help determine the necessity and the effectiveness of planning for your venture? Thurston suggests the following:

• Administrative style and ability—the capability of the CEO to grasp multiple, interrelated aspects of the business.
Some entrepreneurs can keep it all in their heads and retrieve it in an orderly fashion.

• Extent to which the management team wishes to participate in the planning process.

• Complexity of the business—the simpler it is the less the need for formal planning.

• Strength of competition—if your venture needs to be lean, hungry and tightly disciplined in order to compete and to survive, a coherent planning process is important.

• Level of uncertainty—if you are in a volatile, rapidly changing industry, contingency planning may be more important to survival— and preferable to precipitous action—than if you are in a stable, fairly predictable industry.

To these helpful points can be added the notion of "external and other constituencies," including creditors, shareholders, regulators, customers, community, employee groups and the like. The more of these you have to juggle, respond to and contend with, the greater the potential payoff in some form of organized and disciplined planning.

---

1 Phillip Thurston, "Should Smaller Companies Make Formal Plans?", *Harvard Business Review*, Sept–Oct 1983.

2

Getting Ready

When an entrepreneur prepares a business plan he or she must organize and communicate, in writing, the results and conclusions of an analysis of a venture's potential. Few entrepreneurs are good at doing this, even those who have been through a graduate school of business.

To help you develop a good business plan, see the guidelines for preparing a business plan at the end of the book. These guidelines are based on experience in reviewing a large number of business plans, as well as inputs and critiques from leading venture capitalists. Intelligent use of the guidelines should result in a complete and professional business plan, with the information and orderly presentation necessary to interest a venture capitalist.

Be sure to get your team members to prepare those sections of the business plan in their areas of expertise, and to collaborate on any sections that require inputs from several business functions—for example, the manufacturing and operations parts of a plan will require marketing and product design data.

Because the guidelines apply to a wide range of product and service businesses, strict compliance with all aspects of the guidelines is neither possible nor desirable. Common sense should be used in applying the guidelines to your specific venture. As an example: a plan for a service business need not include a section on manufacturing nor, possibly, product development. Further, the guidelines are meant to develop business plans for service or product ventures that have the potential to become substantial companies.

The guidelines are overkill for marginal or "mom and pop" businesses that start and remain small (small motels, retail stores, machine shops or electronic assemblers, for instance). These businesses are generally not of interest to venture capital or other outside investors and do not require a comprehensive business plan. However, readers interested in these kinds of businesses can and should use selected parts of the guidelines to establish the viability of their proposed venture and to develop supporting data for bank-loan applications, particularly the management group, the marketing plan and the cash-flow analysis.

What is in the Guidelines

In the guidelines, there are no questions. The intent is to show you what should be included in a business plan and why. The issues that you should address in your business plan are spelled out. A sequence and structure is given to you, along with explanations where appropriate.

Statements made in a business plan are written with the idea of inducing someone to part with a few hundred thousand dollars, one to two million dollars, or more. This means the statements that you make must be unambiguous and supported. For the purpose of an initial screen it may be all right to say, "The size of the target market for our product is in the $30 to $60 million range and it is growing at over 15% per year."

In a business plan, that sentence would not get by. The size range would need to be narrowed considerably, or the reader will have little confidence in this critical number. Secondly, the phrase "is growing at over 15%" is vague. Does that mean the market grew at that rate between last year and the year before, or on that average over the past three years? Thirdly, "over 15%" is not precise. If you know what the actual growth rate is, say so, and also explain why it will or will not remain the same. If you don't know what the rate is and how it is changing, find out.

Statements in a business plan are taken very seriously by the investor-reader, so you should be able to back them up and defend them. If you are not able to do so, you will lose credibility with an investor. What is more, if you eventually raise outside capital, the investment agreement you will execute with investors legally commits and binds you to the veracity of your statements in the business plan. Any cavalier treatment or misrepresentation can prove to be disasterous, especially if sales don't materialize.

What is Not in the Guidelines

For those contemplating a new venture in any particular industry or market, there are certain to be a number of special, currently critical issues with which they must deal. You should make whatever investigations are needed to develop a list of any special issues likely to affect your venture and industry.

In the chemical industry, for example, some special issues of significance at the present time are: Increasingly strict regulations, at all government levels, covering the use of chemical products and the operation of processes. Diminishing viability of the high capital cost, special-purpose chemical processing plant serving a narrow market. Long delivery times of processing equipment. In the electronics industry, special issues may include future availability and price of new kinds of large-scale integrated circuits.

Each industry has a number of special problems and opportunities. If your company is to enter and maintain a position in an industry, you must know what these problems and opportunities are. You will not find them treated in the general-purpose business plan guidelines: you must find them out for yourself. The guidelines help because they require you to examine carefully a number of potentially relevant issues, but it is up to you to determine which issues are significant to your venture.

Action Steps for Preparing a Business Plan

List all tasks that must be accomplished to prepare your business plan, starting the first week and for four to six weeks thereafter, or whatever relevant time frame you believe is necessary to complete the plan. Here are suggested headings for your list:

Action Steps   *Priority*   *Completion Date*   *Person Responsible*

List each task in as specific and detailed form as possible. Break them down to phone calls, meetings, trips, reports to be written, etc. Try to think of the small tasks that have to happen before a major task can be accomplished (for instance, a trip may be a task, but a series of phone calls may be necessary two weeks earlier to set up the trip). Show who is responsible for each task and when that task will be completed.

Be as specific as possible, and be on the alert for conflicts and lack of reality in your time estimates. Are there any conflicts with you or your associates, other business, or personal activities? Does each of your team members have enough time to accomplish the tasks for which he or she is responsible? Do you have access to critical peole, information, other contacts and resources required to do the job?

Preparing to Write a Business Plan

Here are some important general do's and don'ts for preparing business plans that are worth keeping in mind as you begin to write your own plan. These do's and don'ts have come from experience and reactions to a great many business plans, as well as some of what has been published on the foibles, pet hates, and preferences of venture capitalists.[1]

• Do keep the business plan as short as you can without compromising the description of your venture and its potential. Cover the key issues that will interest an investor and leave the details of secondary importance for a meeting with the investor.

• Do try to say what your business is in fifty words or less. Can you tell the gist of your story in 20–30 pages or 20–30 minutes?

• Don't overdiversify your venture. Focus your attention on one or two product lines and markets. A new or young business does not have the management depth to pursue a number of opportunities.

• Don't have unnamed, mysterious people on your management team—that is, the Mr. G., currently a financial vice president in another firm, who will join you later. The investor will want to know early on exactly who Mr. G. is and what his commitment is.

• Don't describe technical products or manufacturing processes in a way and with a jargon that only an expert can understand. A venture capitalist does not like to invest in what he doesn't understand or thinks you don't understand because you can't explain it clearly to a smart fellow like himself.

---

1 Chas. P. Waite, "The Presentation and Other Key Elements," in *Pratt's Guide to Venture Capital Sources*, 8th ed., Venture Economics, 1984.

• Don't make ambiguous, vague, or unsubstantiated statements. They make you look like a shallow and fuzzy thinker. For example, don't merely say that your markets are growing rapidly. Determine and delineate past, present, and projected future growth rates and market size.

• Don't estimate your sales on the basis of what you can or would like to produce. Do estimate your potential sales carefully, on the basis of your analysis if the marketplace, and then determine the production you need.

• Do disclose and discuss any current or potential problems in your venture. If you fail to do this and the venture capitalist discovers them, your credibility will be badly damaged.

• Do involve all of your management team in the preparation of the business plan as well as any special legal, accounting, or financial help that you may need.

• Don't claim that you have no competition, or indicate that you expect to "get rich quick." Both are good ways to turn off investors, and others, who know better.

• Do recognize that venture capital investors are busy people, and there is not only a need for a short, succinct business plan, but a concise presentation as well. Many venture capital "fairs" and "forums" today, such as those sponsored by Georgia Tech, The Commonwealth of Massachusetts, and the American Electronics Association, require entrepreneurs to present their venture in twenty pages and twenty minutes.

• Don't press for too rapid a decision, or an expression of interest, or conclude too quickly that the investor is ignorant and doesn't understand your business or technology.

• Do explore more than one alternative source of capital financing. There will always be keen competition for the best ventures.

• Don't spend money on developing fancy brochures, elaborate slide show presentations, and other "sizzle." Show the "steak."

• Do be pleasantly persistent and creative in gaining the attention and interest of potential investors.

• Don't assume venture capital is the only, nor necessarily the best, source of funding for your venture. It is suitable mainly for a selective group of ventures of very high potential, which comprise the top one to three percent of all new and emerging businesses.

Getting the Business Plan Reviewed

Once you have written your business plan, you should get it reviewed and critiqued before you submit it to prospective investors. No matter how good you and your team are, there will be issues that you overlook and discussions of aspects of your venture that are inadequate or less than clear. A good reviewer can point these out to you and give you the benefit of an outside, objective evaluation of your plan. A good reviewer can also act as a sounding board to help you develop alternative solutions to some of your venture's problems, and to develop answers to some of the questions that investors are likely to ask.

Who should these reviewers be? One should be an attorney, to make sure that your plan contains no misleading statements, and includes all the information and caveats required in raising money from investors. Other reviewers might be a successful entrepreneur, an entrepreneurially oriented corporate executive who has had significant profit and loss responsibility at or above a divisional level, or a venture capitalist who, for whatever reason, would not be a potential investor in your business. There are also very experienced partners in the Big Eight accounting firms who specialize in privately owned and emerging or entrepreneurial businesses who can provide this service, often at very reasonable rates.

Some Common Omissions and Shortcomings

A number of shortcomings often appear in business plans which tend to turn off prospective investors:

- An entrepreneur who believes that writing a plan is more important than getting orders and generating a positive cash flow.
- "Window-dressing" advisors or board members, such as celebrities, politicians, academics or others who may add recognition or prestige, but actually do nothing.
- Equal stock ownership among the founders.
- Lack of relevant experience and track record in the technology, market-

place and know-how crucial for success in the business.
- An entrepreneur who has fallen in love with the idea for a product or service (my colleague Neil Churchill calls them EIHs, or "entrepreneurs in heat").
- "Hockey stick" sales forecast curves (e.g., "we'll be at $50 million in five years") without much discussion of user benefits, rate of acceptance or economic payback.
- Underestimating the speed, ferocity and vindictiveness of competitors, or ignoring them.
- A "shotgun, cherry-picking" marketing or sales plan without concentration on a niche.
- Succumbing to "spreadsheet diarrhea," or multiple financial scenarios.
- Using accrual-based accounting statements rather than real-time cash-flow projections based on all anticipated actual receipts and disbursements.
- Not spelling out specific assumptions behind revenue, costs, cash flow, timing and rates of increase in staffing, inventory and sales.
- Underestimating costs, lead times and learning curves while overestimating revenues and profits.
- No specific discussion of how the proceeds from the investment or loan will be used, and for what.
- No proposed financing structure, including amount, shares, price and portion of the company to be sold.
- A deal proposal that is insensitive to rate of return and other requirements of the investor or lender.
- Risks ignored or cavalierly dismissed.
- A presentation that is all "big hat and no cattle"—glib, slick and hard sell, seemingly with all the answers but no convincing backup.
- Not forthright, i.e., that covers up, ignores or glosses over bad news, problems or impending liabilities and failures.

What Turns Investors On?

There are five significant risk reducers or return enhancers that excite investors:
- A top-notch, proven and experienced management team.

- Evidence of customer acceptance, such as a sales backlog, orders, letters of serious intent, even trial sites.
- Evidence of a focus and market niche.
- A proprietary or exclusive position created by a license, contract, patent, copyright, etc.
- Appreciation of the investor's goals and requirements.

3

Preparing Financial Statements

by William D. Bygrave

This chapter is a set of instructions for preparing income statements, cash-flow statements, and balance sheets for business plans: income statements and cash flows month-by-month for the first two years, then quarter-by-quarter for the next three years, and balance sheets year-by-year for the first five years.

The statements should fill no more than four pages of 14-column by 66-row spreadsheets, if income and cash flow statements are put on the same page. Pages 1 and 2 would be income and cash flow statements for years 1 and 2, month-by-month. Page 3 would be income and cash flow statements quarter-by-quarter for years 3–5. Page 4 would show balance sheets for all five years, year-by-year.

It is very important to present business-plan financials as clearly and concisely as possible. Sloppy preparation or presentation of financials can ruin a whole business plan.

The model financial statements took about eight hours to prepare with a computer spreadsheet program. They are a set of financial statements for Bygrave and Schuman, Inc., a start-up business to manufacture bicycles for yuppies, college professors and other circus acts.

Step-by-Step Instructions

1. Start with the income statement (Exhibit 1).
a) Determine monthly sales revenue.
b) Determine the cost of goods sold (CGS). Remember that CGS in any period must be the cost only of the goods actually sold in that period.

William D. Bygrave is Associate Professor of Entrepreneurial Studies and Management, and head of the undergraduate program in Entrepreneurial Studies, at Babson College in Wellesley, Massachusetts.

d) Determine overhead costs. Do not include interest or income tax at this point. Wait until you have made a first estimate of cash flow, so you know how much money you need to borrow and the interest rate you will have to pay.

2. Now go to the cash-flow statement (Exhibit 2).

a) This is a real-time (on the calendar) cash-flow statement, not a formal "sources and uses of funds" statement. A real-time cash flow statement is done by asking two simple questions: When will the company receive payments for its goods and services? When will the company pay its wages, its bills, its interest, its taxes, etc.?

b) Start with beginning cash (always $0 for a start-up).

c) Add any equity paid in at the start up. Don't put in any money from a bank loan at this point. The amount you need to borrow will determined from first cash-flow projections.

d) Add any revenue the company expects to receive in actual cash or checks. Not accounts receivable; you can't spend them.

e) Now subtract cash that flows out. At first, record only payments for which checks or cash leave the company. Don't fool with accruals and deferrals. Record wages and salaries actually paid. To keep things simple (and conservative), also record payroll taxes and corporate income taxes in the month they become due.

f) Don't include interest and income taxes in this first cash-flow statement. You don't yet know how much you will need to borrow.

g) You now have ending cash, which becomes beginning cash for the next period.

3. Now determine how much money you need to borrow.

If you look at the cash flow statement of Exhibit 2, you see that the largest ending cash shortfall is $244,000, at the end of April. Bygrave's VP for finance wanted to go through more iterations of income statement and cash flow in order to come up with an exact amount needed. Bygrave said, "Cut that out. $300,000 should be enough. Bankers like round numbers, and it would leave $50,000 for contingencies." So they borrowed $300,000 at 12%.

4. Return to the income statement (Exhibit 3).

a) Write in the monthly interest payments due on the bank loan.

b) Determine the profit before taxes (PBT).

c) Estimate corporate income tax. Don't forget the losses to be carried forward. If you want to be precise with your tax estimates, ask an accountant for the current tax schedules.

d) You have now completed the income statement.

5. Return to the cash-flow statement (Exhibit 4).

a) Put the interest and income-tax payments into the cash-flow projections.

b) You have now completed the cash-flow statement. Note that the lowest cash balance for Bygrave is $44,000 at the end of April—if all goes according to plan. If it doesn't, this will be a good safety cushion.

6. Now for the balance sheets (Exhibit 5).

a) Cash is the ending cash balance on December 31.

b) Accounts receivable are those outstanding on December 31. At Bygrave, they are the sales revenue calculated for the bicycles shipped in December.

c) Inventory is taken on December 31. At Bygrave, it is the bicycles manufactured in December.

d) Assets for Bygrave are the $9,000 deposit for three months rent, and deposits to the telephone and electric companies totalling $2,000.

e) Accounts payable are the $15,000 due for materials delivered in December, since Bygrave pays for its materials in the month after they are delivered.

f) Bank loan. Split this into the amount due during the next 12 months (a current liability) and the balance due after that (a long-term liability).

g) Paid-in equity is the total equity paid in by stockholders.

h) Retained earnings (losses) is the accumulated earnings (losses) from the inception of the company through the date of the balance sheet. For Bygrave, this is the net income for the first year, $80,000.

EXHIBIT 1

Bygrave & Schuman, Inc.
INCOME STATEMENT, 1989 ($1,000)

	Jan	Feb	Mar	Apr	May	Jun	Jul	Aug	Sep	Oct	Nov	Dec	YEAR
REVENUE	$0	$100	$150	$200	$200	$150	$100	$50	$100	$100	$200	$100	$1,450
Material	0	15	23	30	30	23	15	8	15	15	30	15	219
Labor	0	30	45	60	60	45	30	15	30	30	60	30	435
Rent, bldg.	0	2	2	2	2	2	2	2	2	2	2	2	22
Rent, equip.	0	2	2	2	2	2	2	2	2	2	2	2	22
TOTAL CGS	0	49	72	94	94	72	49	27	49	49	94	49	698
GROSS INCOME	$0	$51	$78	$106	$106	$78	$51	$23	$51	$51	$106	$51	$752
Salaries	20	20	20	20	20	20	20	20	20	20	20	20	240
Marketing	20	20	20	20	20	20	20	20	20	20	20	20	210
Utilities	5	5	5	5	5	5	5	5	5	5	5	5	60
Insurance	4	4	4	4	4	4	4	4	4	4	4	4	48
Rent, office	1	1	1	1	1	1	1	1	1	1	1	1	12
Autos	1	1	1	1	1	1	1	1	1	1	1	1	12
Travel	2	2	2	2	2	2	2	2	2	2	2	2	24
Entertainment	1	1	1	1	1	1	1	1	1	1	1	1	12
TOTAL GA&S	54	54	54	54	54	54	39	39	54	54	54	54	618
PBIT	($54)	($3)	$24	$52	$52	$24	$12	($16)	($3)	($3)	$52	($3)	$134
Interest													
PBT													
Income tax													
NET INCOME													

EXHIBIT 2

Bygrave & Schuman, Inc.
CASH FLOW, 1989 ($1,000)

	Jan	Feb	Mar	Apr	May	Jun	Jul	Aug	Sep	Oct	Nov	Dec
BEGIN CASH	$0	($87)	($201)	($238)	($244)	($173)	($80)	($11)	$12	($37)	($78)	($92)
Bank loan												
Equity paid in	20											
Revenue	0	0	100	150	200	200	150	100	50	100	100	200
TOTAL CASH IN	$20	$0	$100	$150	$200	$200	$150	$100	$50	$100	$100	$200
Material	0	15	23	30	30	23	15	8	15	15	30	15
Labor	30	45	60	60	45	30	15	30	30	60	30	30
Rent, building	8	2	2	2	2	2	2	2	2	2	2	2
Rent, equipment	2	2	2	2	2	2	2	2	2	2	2	2
Salaries	20	20	20	20	20	20	20	20	20	20	20	20
Marketing	20	20	20	20	20	20	5	5	20	20	20	20
Utilities	7	5	5	5	5	5	5	5	5	5	5	5
Insurance	12			12			12			12		
Rent, office	4	1	1	1	1	1	1	1	1	1	1	1
Autos	1	1	1	1	1	1	1	1	1	1	1	1
Travel	2	2	2	2	2	2	2	2	2	2	2	2
Entertainment	1	1	1	1	1	1	1	1	1	1	1	1
TOTAL CASH OUT	107	114	137	156	129	107	81	77	99	141	114	99
ENDING CASH	($87)	($201)	($238)	($244)	($173)	($80)	($11)	$12	($37)	($78)	($92)	$9

EXHIBIT 3

Bygrave & Schuman, Inc.
INCOME STATEMENT, 1989 ($1,000)

	Jan	Feb	Mar	Apr	May	Jun	Jul	Aug	Sep	Oct	Nov	Dec	YEAR
REVENUE	$0	$100	$150	$200	$200	$150	$100	$50	$100	$100	$200	$100	$1,450
Material	0	15	23	30	30	23	15	8	15	15	30	15	219
Labor	0	30	45	60	60	45	30	15	30	30	60	30	435
Rent, bldg.	0	2	2	2	2	2	2	2	2	2	2	2	22
Rent, equip.	0	2	2	2	2	2	2	2	2	2	2	2	22
TOTAL CGS	0	49	72	94	94	72	49	27	49	49	94	49	698
GROSS INCOME	$0	$51	$78	$106	$106	$78	$51	$23	$51	$51	$106	$51	$752
Salaries	20	20	20	20	20	20	20	20	20	20	20	20	240
Marketing	20	20	20	20	20	20	5	5	20	20	20	20	210
Utilities	5	5	5	5	5	5	5	5	5	5	5	5	60
Insurance	4	4	4	4	4	4	4	4	4	4	4	4	48
Rent, office	1	1	1	1	1	1	1	1	1	1	1	1	12
Autos	1	1	1	1	1	1	1	1	1	1	1	1	12
Travel	2	2	2	2	2	2	2	2	2	2	2	2	24
Entertainment	1	1	1	1	1	1	1	1	1	1	1	1	12
TOTAL GA&S	54	54	54	54	54	54	39	39	54	54	54	54	618
PBI&T	($54)	($3)	$24	$52	$52	$24	$12	($16)	($3)	($3)	$52	($3)	$134
Interest	3	3	3	3	3	3	3	3	3	3	3	3	36
PBT	($57)	($6)	$21	$49	$49	$21	$9	($19)	($6)	($6)	$49	($6)	$98
Income tax	0	0	0	0	8	5	2	0	0	0	5	0	$20
NET INCOME	($57)	($6)	$21	$49	$41	$16	$7	($19)	($6)	($6)	$44	($6)	$78

EXHIBIT 4

Bygrave & Schuman, Inc.
CASH FLOW, 1989 ($1,000)

	Jan	Feb	Mar	Apr	May	Jun	Jul	Aug	Sep	Oct	Nov	Dec
BEGIN CASH	$0	$210	$93	$53	$44	$104	$189	$253	$273	$221	$177	$155
Bank loan	300											
Equity paid in	20											
Revenue	0	0	100	150	200	200	150	100	50	100	100	200
TOTAL CASH IN	$320	$0	$100	$150	$200	$200	$150	$100	$50	$100	$100	$200
Material	30	15	23	30	30	23	15	8	15	15	30	15
Labor	30	45	60	60	45	30	15	30	30	60	30	30
Rent, building	8	2	2	2	2	2	2	2	2	2	2	2
Rent, equipment	2	2	2	2	2	2	2	2	2	2	2	2
Salaries	20	20	20	20	20	20	20	20	20	20	20	20
Marketing	20	20	20	20	20	20	5	5	20	20	20	20
Utilities	7	5	5	5	5	5	5	5	5	5	5	5
Insurance	12			12			12			12		
Rent, office	4	1	1	1	1	1	1	1	1	1	1	1
Autos	1	1	1	1	1	1	1	1	1	1	1	1
Travel	2	2	2	2	2	2	2	2	2	2	2	2
Entertainment	1	1	1	1	1	1	1	1	1	1	1	1
Interest	3	3	3	3	3	3	3	3	3	3	3	3
Income tax	0	0	0	0	8	5	2	0	0	0	5	0
TOTAL CASH OUT	110	117	140	159	140	115	86	80	102	144	122	102
ENDING CASH	$210	$93	$53	$44	$104	$189	$253	$273	$221	$177	$155	$253

EXHIBIT 5

Bygrave & Schuman, Inc.
BALANCE SHEET
Years Ending Dec 31 ($1,000)

	1989	*1990*	*1991*	*1992*	*1993*
ASSETS					
Current					
Cash	255				
A/R	100				
Inventory	49				
Rent deposit	9				
Utilities deposit	2				
TOTAL	**$415**				
LIABILITIES					
Current					
A/P	15				
Bank loan	60				
Long-term					
Bank loan	240				
Equity paid in	20				
Retained earnings	80				
TOTAL	**$415**				

Footnotes:
(1) Wages and salaries are paid in month earned (no accruals).
(2) Materials are paid for on the month after purchase.
(3) Finished goods are shipped and booked as sales
    in the month after they are manufactured.
(4) Payment terms are net 30 days—A/R equal revenue
    in the prior month.
(5) There are prepaid deposits for rent and utilties.
(6) Insurance is paid quarterly.
(7) Income tax is paid in the current month (no accruals
    or deferrals).
(8) Loan is to be repaid in years 1–6.
(9) Ending inventory is the CGS in the following month,
    i.e., goods manufactured in the current month are sold
    in the next month.

4

Financing the Venture:
Navigating Uncharted Waters

It has taken over ten years, a lot of sweat equity, many sleepless nights and personal guarantees on company bank loans to build your firm to $5 million in sales. Profits have been up and down as a result of spending current income to grow, but you are confident that the firm can exceed $11 million quite profitable sales by 1992. But growing a company requires cash.

By early 1988, your banker—and ten other banks you have approached—says "no" to your request to extend your line of credit from $500,000 to $1.5 million to help fund your growth plans. Unless you can raise more equity for the business, which you personally do not have, the banks are going to pass.

You meet a lawyer at a seminar for entrepreneurs who insists he can take you public in Vancouver or London and raise $2.5 million. That sounds like good news. After all, that would dramatically improve your balance sheet and provide the cash you sorely need for expansion. Then you figure out the cost: the lawyers, underwriters, accountants, printers and regulators will require a total of 35% of the total offering off the top! Is this your only alternative?

You've spent the last dozen years building your firm from scratch to $50 million in sales with a solid record of profitable growth in recent years. Although the firm is still small by Fortune 500 standards, you have become the dominant firm in your industry. Given your plans for continued growth, you and your backers and directors decide the timing is right for an initial public offering (IPO) of the company's stock. Fortunately, the underwriters agree.

Four months later everything is on schedule and the "road shows" to present your company to the various offices of your underwriter are scheduled to begin the following month—October 1987. The rest is history.

These two entrepreneurs have at least one thing in common: they are sailing in unfamiliar waters, and they may not have a compass or the right chart. Even in good times the financial domain for most smaller company presidents—by their own admission—is the least familiar and most feared territory. Lack of any technical education or first-hand knowledge and experience with financing is common. And many small company entrepreneurs do not have a working relationship with a venture capitalist, investment banker, "angels" or even a financial advisor they rely on as an impartial, friendly advocate.

What do such entrepreneurs do about their fund-raising strategies? The wisdom of the saying, "There ain't no such thing as a free lunch," applies particularly to financing. Knowing what you are getting into, and what risks and trade-offs to look—and look out—for is often every bit as important as how much money you get and from whom. For the entrepreneur, these issues and risks are not generally advertised nor visible in advance. Developing a fund-raising strategy and obtaining funding can a minefield, especially for the unititated. Why is this so?

A fund-raising strategy commits the company to actions that incur costs and take real time, which may enhance or inhibit future financing efforts. Similarly, each source of funding has particular requirements and costs—both apparent and hidden—with implications for the future of a company. The serious risks to consider are the consequences of both the strategy and the source. Savvy entrepreneurs are aware of the potential for punishment in raising money. They pay attention to the details with a certain wariness as they evaluate, select, negotiate and develop business relationships with funding sources. In doing so, they are more likely to find the right sources, at the right time and on the right terms and conditions—and avoid costly mismatches.

The stock-market crash in October 1987 has significantly raised the level of caution in the financial markets and institutions serving smaller companies, as lenders and investors alike seek to reduce risk. Are there alternatives to conventional financing today? If so, what are they, and where do you turn without getting burned? What are some these potentially fatal attractions? How do you avoid the lure of unconventional sources of cash that turn out to be Venus flytraps? What are some of the issues and considerations in recognizing and avoiding them, while devising a fund-raising strategy and evaluating and negotiating with various sources of funds?

Being able to recognize these realities and dangers—and to respond appropriately—depends on an understanding of the "financial life cycle" and an ability to spot the Venus flytraps that await. Fortunately, there is every indication that significant amounts of capital are available through private sources of funds. The saying, "Too much money chasing too few deals," is alive and well.

The Financial Life Cycle and Sources of Equity

Depending on your goals and needs—growth, control, liquidity, estate building or even harvesting—you have many choices among financing alternatives. Which ones are best for you, or even available, will depend on your company's circumstances and stage of growth, the industry and, most important, your personal goals. One key question for owners: do you really want outside partners? If the answer is "yes," which sources are the most sensible to pursue?

One way to begin answering this question is to appreciate the financial life cycle of a firm. The graph on the next page shows the principal sources of risk capital for pre start-up, new and growing firms. Each source has different preferences and practices, including how much money they will provide, when in a company's life cycle they will invest, and the cost of the capital: the expected rate of return (ROR) they are seeking.

The available sources of capital change dramatically for companies at different stages and rates of growth, and as one company moves through different stages. One can see that many of the sources of equity are not available until the company progresses beyond the earlier stages.

Conversely, some of the sources available to early-stage companies, especially personal sources, friends and other informal investors or "angels," will be insufficient to meet the financing requirements generated in later stages, if the company continues to grow successfully.

In general, the younger the company the riskier the investment. While the time line and dollar limits shown are only guidelines, they do reflect how these money sources view the riskiness, and thus the required rate of return, of companies at various stages of development. These guidelines change with the current market and may vary in different areas of the country from time to time.

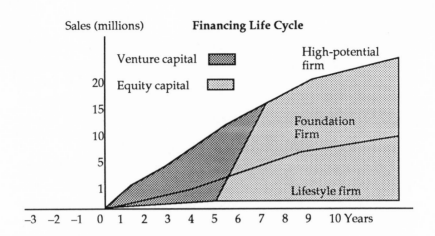

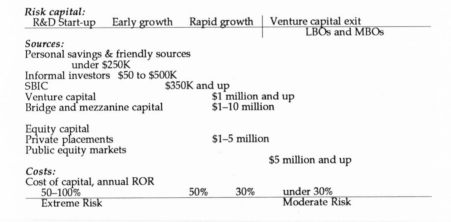

Another key factor affecting the availability of financing is the potential of the company. High-potential firms, those that grow rapidly and are likely to exceed $15 to $20 million or more in sales, and thus become strong prospects for an IPO, have the widest array of financing alternatives. Of the more than one million new businesses launched each year, no more than 5% will achieve such a growth and sales level. The "foundation firms," 8–12% of all new firms, will grow more slowly but exceed $1 million in sales and may grow to $5–15 million. The remaining are the traditional, stable small businesses and lifestyle firms.

Debt Sources

A similar pattern exists among the various debt alternatives available, with one important distinction: it is nearly impossible for a start-up to obtain a bank loan unless it has a significant amount of initial equity money, since banks lend almost exclusively to existing businesses with identifiable cash flow and collateral. Table 1 summarizes the leading sources for new and existing firms.

Table 1 What is bankable? Specific lending criteria:

Security	Credit capacity
Accounts receivable	70–80% those less than 90 days
Inventory	40–60%, depending on obsolescence risk
Equipment	70–80% of market value (less if specialized)
Chattel mortgage	100–150% + of auction appraisal value
Conditional sales contract	60–70% + of purchase price
Plant improvement loan	60–80% of appraised value or cost

The advantages and disadvantages of these sources are basically determined by such obvious dimensions as the interest rate or cost of capital, the key terms, conditions and covenants, and the fit with the owner's situation and the company's needs at the time. How good a deal you can strike is in turn a function of your relative bargaining position and the competitiveness among the alternatives.

What is ultimately most important, given a deal at or above an acceptable threshold, is the person you will be dealing with, rather than the amount, terms or institution. In other words, you will be better off seeking the right banker (or other provider of capital) than just the right bank. Once again, the industry and market characteristics, stage and health of the firm in terms of cash flow, debt coverage and collateral are central to the evaluation process.

Table 2 summarizes the term of financing available from these different sources. Note the difficulty in finding sources for more than one year of financing.

Finally, an enduring question entrepreneurs ask is, What is bankable? How much money can I expect to borrow based on my balance sheet? Table 3 summarizes some some general guidelines in answer to this question.

Table 2 Debt financing sources for types of business

Source	Start-up company	Existing company
Trade credit	Yes	Yes
Commercial banks	Occasionally, with strong equity	Yes
Finance companies	Rare (if assets are available)	Yes
Factors	Rare	Yes
Leasing companies	Difficult, except for start-ups with venture capital	Yes
Mutual savings banks, S&Ls	Rare	Real estate and other asset-based companies
Insurance companies	Rare, except alongside venture capital	Yes

Table 3 Debt financing sources by term of financing

Source	Term of financing		
	Short	Medium	Long
Trade credit	Yes	Yes	Possible
Commercial banks	Most frequently	Yes (asset-based)	Rare (depends onasset)
Factors	Most frequently	Rare	No
Leasing companies	No	Most frequently	Some
Mutual savings banks, S&Ls	No	No	Real estate and other asset-based companies
Insurance companies	Rare	More frequently	Yes

5

Sources of Capital

Money is like a sixth sense without which you cannot make a complete use of the other five.

Somerset Maugham, *Of Human Bondage*

Every entrepreneur must eventually take on the job of raising money to start, expand or buy a business, or to provide funds for seasonal or temporary business needs. Many sources of financing and types of capital are available. Some can be used to finance a start-up. Others can only be used to provide capital for a going concern. For example, start-ups may only be able to obtain money from friends, relatives and certain venture capital groups oriented to financing new ventures. On the other hand, existing businesses have a far wider range of financing options available to them, which include banks, commercial finance companies, leasing companies, public sale of stock, and venture capital firms.

Debt versus Equity
Generally speaking, a company's operations can be financed through debt and through some form of equity financing.[1] Short-term debt (one year or less) is required by a business for working capital, and is repaid out of the proceeds of its sales.

Longer term borrowings (term loans of one to five years or long-term loans maturing in more than five years) are used for working capital and/or to finance the purchase of property or equipment that serve as collateral for the loan. The most common sources of such debt financing are commercial banks.

---

1 In addition to common stock, equity financing is meant to include both stock and subordinated debt, or subordinated debt with stock conversion features, or warrants to purchase stock.

However, the new venture just starting has difficulty obtaining either short- or longer term bank debt without a substantial cushion of equity financing, or long-term debt subordinated[2] to all bank debt.

As a rule of thumb, a start-up may be able to obtain debt for working capital equal to its equity and subordinated debt. Without much equity capital or subordinated debt, the new venture will not be able to obtain much bank debt. As far as the bank is concerned, a start-up has little proven capability to generate the sales, profits, and cash to pay off short-term debt, and even less ability to sustain profitable operations over a number of years and retire long-term debt.

Even using a venture's assets as loan collateral may be insufficient to obtain bank loans. Asset values can erode with time and, in the absence of adequate equity capital and demonstrated good management, may provide little real loan security to a bank.

This is not to say that a start-up cannot obtain credit and loans. Sometimes a new venture can obtain long-term financing for a piece of equipment from its manufacturer, who will accept part of the purchase price as a long-term note. Manufacturers are willing to do this if there is an active market for their used equipment, in the event of a default.

Long-term debt for a venture might be obtained from a bank if a loan guarantee for 90% of the loan can be obtained from the SBA (Small Business Administration). However, the SBA does require that the loans it guarantees be sound or secured. Many new businesses fail to qualify for SBA guarantees.

A new business can also try to reduce its need for long-term debt by leasing some of the equipment it needs. Such leases may be provided by a manufacturer or by a commercial credit company. Until recently, leasing was usually restricted to general-purpose equipment (e.g., oscilloscopes, fork lifts) for which there is a strong demand. However, several leasing companies have recently introduced programs to lease more specialized equipment to high-technology start-ups that have

2 Venture capital investors normally subordinate their business loans to the loans provided by a bank or other financial institutions. Commercial banks regard such subordinated debt as equity.

obtained equity financing from venture capital groups. To compensate for the greater risk, these companies also receive stock purchase warrants in addition to typical leasing interest rates.

A start-up can sometimes obtain short-term debt financing by negotiating extended credit terms with one or more of its suppliers. A disadvantage of this kind of trade credit is that it restricts the flexibility of the venture to select suppliers, and reduces the venture's ability to negotiate supplier prices.

An existing business has a much easier job obtaining debt and equity. Banks, leasing companies, and finance companies will often seek out such companies, and regard them as important customers for secured and unsecured short and term loans. Furthermore, an existing and expanding business finds it easier to raise equity capital from private or institutional sources and on better terms than a start-up.

Although it may be possible to finance a venture with a great deal of debt and little equity capital, there can be a number of disadvantages in doing this. A new and growing company is a consumer of capital and is ill able to afford the regular payments of interest and principal required with debt financing. Many new ventures that are predominantly debt-financed (i.e., heavily leveraged), are constantly undercapitalized and have continual cash flow problems.

Cash flow problems can occupy the time and attention of the venture's management to the detriment of the general development and growth of the venture. Also, the heavy use of debt for starting or expanding a company can adversely affect the venture's balance sheet and its ability to obtain future debt or equity financing at favorable terms.

On the positive side, debt financing does not dilute the entrepreneurs' equity, and the leverage it provides can increase the return on invested capital. But remember that leverage works both ways. In times of tight credit and high interest rates, a business with a high debt-to-equity ratio is much more likely to have financial difficulty or even be driven into bankruptcy than businesses with more reasonable capitalizations.

An otherwise successful consumer products company with sales of $30 million over-leveraged its debt (e.g., its debt was eight times equity) and was driven into *bankruptcy by the combined effects of rising interest rates and a recession-induced drop in sales.*

A new or existing business must obtain both equity and debt financing if it is to have a sound financial foundation for growth without excessive dilution of the entrepreneurs' equity.

This and the following chapters answer such questions as: What are the sources of short, medium and long-term financing? What sources provide capital for start-ups? For existing businesses? What are the financing limits and investment preferences of the various sources? What data must be submitted to obtain financing? What terms and conditions can be expected on particular financings? What are the advantages and disad-vantages of the various kinds of financing?

Stages and Types of Ventures

From whom does a venture obtain venture or equity capital? The answer to this question depends both on the growth potential of the venture—slow, moderate or fast—and the stage of its development. Attention here is focused on equity capital for the birth and early growth of a venture. Within this time frame are three stages of development where a venture may need capital and obtain it from different kinds of investors.

The *seed stage* of venture development begins with the idea for a business, encompasses the organization and planning of a venture and some research and development, and ends with the creation of a business entity and a business plan.

The *start-up stage* begins when a venture is organized and one or two of its principals begin actively to complete development of its products and to seek sales. The start-up stage ends when the venture can demonstrate commercial interest in its product. The start-up stage can last anywhere from several months to a year, and a venture may not be profitable at the end of it.

First-stage companies are going organizations. There is evidence of commercial interest in their products and some sales. However, profits may be one or more years off.

In addition to stage, the type of firm influences the availability financing.[3] *Life-style firms* are firms with potential annual sales of less than $1 million and managed by people willing to sacrifice income for the life style afforded by running their own small company. These firms have little or no real growth by choice, market size, or circumstance.

Foundation firms are firms with potential sales of $1 million to $20 million and from 30 to 600 employees. These firms grow at one to two times the growth rate of the GNP: 10%-20% per year.

High-potential firms are firms with potential sales of $20 million and growing in excess of 30% per year.

Life-style firms are financed almost entirely by the personal savings of the entrepreneurs, while high-potential firms have a much wider choice of financing alternatives.

Entrepreneurs and their associates may also be expected to provide some of the seed capital for foundation and high-potential firms. This may be in the form of foregone salary while the venture is organized and started and/or in actual cash. Venture capital firms investing in an early-stage venture like the entrepreneurs to have made some sort of significant financial commitment to the venture.

Informal Sources of Venture Capital

In addition to the entrepreneurs and their associates, an important source of seed and start-up funds, and financing at all stages for life-style firms, is found among the personal and professional contacts of the entrepreneurs of new ventures:

Family and friends.

Professional advisers and business acquaintances.

Past employers.

Potential customers and suppliers of the new venture.

Prospective employees (who may invest or be given stock in return for working at less than prevailing compensation).

3 William H. Wetzel, Jr., "The Cost of Availability of Credit and Risk Capital in New England" in *A Region's Struggling Savior: Small Business in New England*, edited by J. Timmons and David Gumpert (The Small Business Foundation of America, Inc., 1979).

Wealthy businessmen and private investors who know the entrepreneurs.

In all, it is estimated that 98–99% of the capital for new businesses comes from these sources.

These people will generally invest in an opportunistic way, without too much study or investigation, and largely on the basis of personal or business relationships with the principals. They can also invest at later stages of a venture's development; but the capital then required will usually exceed what they alone can supply.

The entrepreneur and his management team should review their contacts in the categories listed above and determine whether any of them might be interested in making a financial commitment to the venture. They should take care to know these potential investors well enough to insure that they are not unethical, or only interested in a fast profit with no concern for the entrepreneur or the venture.

A good deal of the early funding for new ventures has been provided by wealthy individuals. This is especially true outside of the centers (Boston, New York, San Francisco) of organized venture capital. There are a number of such people who invest more or less regularly in start-up entrepreneurial efforts. They may do this alone or in syndication with other wealthy individuals, dubbed "angels" by my colleague, Bill Wetzel.[2]

Make no mistake about it, "angels" are probably the single most important source of capital for start-up and emerging businesses in the United States today. Usually they will be knowledgeable and experienced in the market and technology areas where they invest. The right ones will also add a lot more to your business than just money. The savvy, know-how and contacts from having made it themselves they can bring to your business as advisors or directors can be far more valuable than the $20,000 to $50,000 each one may invest.

2 William H. Wetzel, Jr., "Angels and Risk Capital," *Sloan Management Review,* Summer 1983, Vol. 24, No. 4, pp. 23–34.

Most of the capital from "angels" covers financings in the $50,000 to $500,000 range, amounts usually too small for professional venture capital sources. According to Wetzel, there are 250,000 or more such investors in the United States, 100,000 of whom are active. The typical investment is $20,000 to $50,000, with 36% involving less than $10,000, while 24% are for over $50,000. In total, Wetzel believes that these angels invest $5 to $10 billion annually in 20,000 to 30,000 companies. This is staggering in comparison to the 2,500 to 3,000 companies invested in each year by the U. S. venture capital industry.

Who are these "angels" and where can they be found? The answer is that they are mainly self-made entrepreneurial millionaires, nearly two million of them. They have made it on their own and have substantial business and financial experience. Finding them isn't easy. Other successful entrepreneurs know them, as do many tax attorneys and accountants, bankers and other professionals. Invariably, you find them by tapping your own networks of business associates and other contacts.

Generally the evaluation of a potential investment by such investors tends to be less thorough than that undertaken by an organized venture capital group, and non-economic factors (e.g., a desire to be involved with entrepreneurs) may be important to their investment decisions. In the case of a syndicate of such investors, one individual may make the evaluation for the group.

Ex-entrepreneurs who have made money through starting, developing, and selling companies are a good source of start-up capital, as are some wealthy doctors, lawyers, and businessmen. Although these people make start-up investments, they often demand more equity for their interest than the entrepreneur may think reasonable. Some of them may try to dominate the venture, and others can get very impatient when sales and profits don't grow as they expected. To avoid legal problems associated with the sale of stock to such investors, review carefully the material in this book on the legal aspects of a stock offering.

6

Looking for Equity Capital

Entrepreneurs generally find the search for venture (equity) capital to be much more time-consuming, expensive and frustrating than they ever imagined. It is important, therefore, that entrepreneurs understand how to find, select and best present their venture to equity investors— whether "informal sources" of capital (such as professional acquaintances and/or wealthy individuals) or professional venture capital firms.

Before beginning their search for equity capital, entrepreneurs should have completed a logical, comprehensive, and *readable* business plan. It must be long enough to present the potential of a business but not so long as to bore or discourage the investor-reader. The plan prepared for informal investors can generally be less detailed than that prepared for the professional venture capitalist. The entrepreneurs should also have demonstrated their commitment to the venture by investing a significant amount of their time and some of their money in it.

Entrepreneurs should not delay looking for equity capital until they have a serious cash shortage, since it is likely to take six months or more to raise start-up capital, if they have not previously succeeded in doing so. In addition to impairing the development of their venture, the lack of planning implicit in this cash shortage can undermine their credibility as good managers and have a negative impact on their ability to negotiate with investors. Beginning a search for equity when you are out of cash, or nearly so, is to put yourself in one of the worst possible situations for raising money.

On the other hand, if entrepreneurs seek and obtain money before they really need it, they may unnecessarily dilute their own equity, as well as erode, inadvertently, the discipline instilled by financial leanness.

Entrepreneurs should try to anticipate their cash needs, go as far as they deem prudent on their existing capital, and then prepare themselves to raise funds from equity investors. To determine how much money you need, you must prepare cash-flow statements, with the details on revenue, cost and start-up resources that underlie the numbers, as discussed in Chapter 3.

What to Look For

When looking for a venture capital investor, you should seek someone
- who is considering new financing proposals and can provide the required level of capital.
- who is interested in early-stage companies and may already have investments in your customers' industry.
- who has a preference and the know-how for investments in your industry, i.e., who knows your market and your product, technology or service area.
- who has a successful track record building smaller companies, preferably for ten years or more.
- who can provide good business advice, moral support, and contacts in the business and financial community as well as venture capital.
- who has co-invested with quality venture-capital firms and underwriters.
- with whom the entrepreneur gets along.
- who is reputable and ethical.

The best single sourcebook is *Pratt's Guide to Venture Capital Sources*, 13th edition (available from Venture Economics, Needham MA).

Informal Investors

Informal investors are more likely than a professional venture capitalist to invest in companies that are small, risky and with not much potential for liquidity. Typically, such investors may be wealthy individuals and successful entrepreneurs, businessmen, and professionals. Such investors can be an important source of capital for the "seed" or research and development stages of high potential firms and for the early-stage financing of foundation firms. This is especially true in areas of the country that do not have ready access to professional venture capital groups.

Informal investors are particularly appropriate for financing
- high-technology inventors before the development of a prototype.
- ventures with capital requirements of between $50,000 and $500,000.
- ventures with a sales potential five to ten years out of between $2 million and $20 million.
- small but established, privately held ventures whose sales and profit growth (10% to 20% per year) is not rapid enough to be attractive to a professional venture capital firm.[1]

Informal investors often have non-economic factors as well as capital gains in mind when they make their investment decisions. A successful entrepreneur may want to help other entrepreneurs get started. A wealthy individual may want to help build new businesses in his or her community. The typical informal investor will invest from $25,000 to $50,000 in any one venture.

Finding Informal Investors

Apart from serendipity, such investors learn of investment opportunities from their business associates, fellow entrepreneurs and friends, many of whom invest together, more or less regularly, in a number of new venture situations. Thus, one informal investor contact can lead the entrepreneur to others. In New England, the Venture Capital Network in Concord, New Hampshire, has a computerized database for linking entrepreneurs and would-be investors.

The best way to meet informal investors is to seek advice and referrals from attorneys, accountants, business associates and entrepreneurs who deal with new ventures and are likely to know such people. Even the faculty at an entrepreneurs' university can be a source of potential investors. By using the referrer's name, it is generally possible to arrange a meeting with a potential investor. At this meeting the entrepreneur should make a concise presentation of the key features of the proposed venture and his or her qualifications to make it successful.

---

1 William H. Wetzel, Jr., "Angels and Risk Capital," *op. cit.*

Whether or not the outcome of such a meeting is continued invest-ment interest, the entrepreneur should try to obtain the names of other potential investors from this meeting. If this can be done, the entre-preneur will develop a growing list of potential investors and will find his or her way into one or more networks of informal investors. This process is time-consuming and laborious—but it can succeed.

The entrepreneur should avoid meeting with more than one infor-mal investor at the same time. Such meetings often result in negative viewpoints being raised by one investor and reinforced by another. It is also easier to deal with negative reactions and questions from only one investor at a time.

In most cities, there are both law firms and private placement syndicators who put packages together to raise a few hundred thousand to even several million dollars from their networks. Venture magazine publishes a directory of these firms.

There is also an emerging breed of "entrepreneurial company build-ers" who can be an excellent alternative to venture capitalists, especially if you don't want to grow at a breakneck pace, or give up a huge slice of your equity pie. One such firm is the CML Group of Acton, Massachu-setts. They have a "farm-system" concept of providing debt, equity and management know-how to emerging companies, and own such compa-nies Boston Whaler, Carroll Reed Shops, The Nature Company and others.

Informal Investors' Evaluation

More likely than not, more than one meeting will be required to close with potential investors. They will want to review the business plan, meet the full management team, and see any product prototype or design that may exist. They will conduct background checks on the venture team and its product potential, usually through someone they know who knows the entrepreneur and the product. The process is not dissimilar to that done by a professional venture capital firm but may be less formal and structured. Often, the participation of one investor who is knowl-edgeable about the product and its market will trigger the participation of other investors.

Throughout these discussions, you will be selling and negotiating. One good frame of mind to assume is that the deal will not close, and therefore you should always have alternative sources in the wings. This is probably the single most effective way to maximize the value of your equity and to avoid running out of cash before the deal is closed. It is closed when you have deposited the funds and the check has cleared—not a moment sooner.

Once the required financial commitments have been obtained, the investors will have an investment agreement drafted by an attorney. This agreement may be simpler than those used by professional venture capital firms. It may also include some form of a "put" whereby the investors have the right to require the venture to repurchase their stock after a specified number of years at a specified price. If the venture becomes a lifestyle firm, this "put" will provide the investors with a cash return and satisfies the lifestyle entrepreneur's desire for complete control of the venture.

What to Look Out For

In doing your own investigations, you will want to be especially alert to any of the following warning signs, and avoid such backers, unless you are so desperate that you have no real alternatives.

• You can't get through to one of the general partners to make your case—only a junior associate or assistant seems to be interested.

• The general partner who will be a director in your company also sits on the board of seven or more other start-ups and early stage companies, and may in the midst of raising yet another fund.

• The partner you will deal with has an MBA from a top business school, has no operating or start-up experience, is thirty or younger and has only worked on Wall Street prior to attaining the MBA—or has some equivalently narrow and overly financial focus.

• The fund has a reputation for frequently replacing founders.

• More than one fourth of the companies in the fund's portfolio are in trouble, i.e., failing to meet their business-plan targets.

• The partners are known for their "get rich quick" philosophy, rather than their patience and bravery.

• The partners think they can run your business better than you can.

7

Professional Venture Capital

The 1980s have seen a metamorphosis in the professional venture capital industry. The reduction in capital gains taxes led to an explosion of new money in 1979, and by 1989 there is eighty times as much new venture capital available as there was ten to fifteen years ago; in fact, some say that "too much capital is chasing too few good deals." In 1987, for example, over $4 billion of new capital was invested, and most of this after the stock-market crash of October. A similar amount was invested in 1988, according to the *Venture Capital Journal*.

Of equal significance is the amount of money being invested in start-ups. In the middle 1970s, only 14% of investments were in start-ups. In the early 1980s, 90% of venture capital firms reported that they would consider investing in start-ups. Leading this trend were eight venture capital firms that specialize in start-ups and very early stage ventures; they reported that half or more of their investments were in start-up companies. By the late 1980s nearly one quarter of all investments were in seed and start-up firms.

Some venture capital firms become actively involved financially and managerially in the seed stage of new ventures. Rather than wait for a deal to come to them, they decide on a product or technology they wish to commercialize and put their own deal together. This involves assembling a team of entrepreneurs, managers and technologists, writing business plans, troubleshooting the venture and providing seed capital alone or in syndication with other venture capital firms.

Take, for example, Zero Stage Capital, a small fund specializing in seed-stage innovators. They will invest as little as $50,000 in a one-person operation for the development of a prototype to determine if the concept works. If it does, they will then invest a second round to fund the development of a business and marketing plan and to attract a key management team member. These staged investments enable the enterprise to move ahead, based on acccomplishments and promise, without overfunding the venture.

Sometimes these seed deals are organized as equity partnerships rather than corporations (see the discussion of tax shelters). An equity partnership allows the early losses of the venture to flow directly back to the limited-partner investors. This gives the investors a tax deduction, which reduces their capital at risk, in return for which the entrepreneurs get to keep more equity than they would in a corporate seed venture.

Capital from a professional venture capital group is very attractive to the entrepreneur. The venture capitalist can bring more than just money to the venture: he or she brings the experience of having done it before. Moreover, the venture firm has "deep pockets," and contacts with other groups to facilitate raising of money as the venture develops.

However, professional venture capital groups have stringent criteria for their investments. They look for ventures with very high growth potential where they can quintuple their investment in five years. Venture capital firms also place a high premium on the quality of the management in a venture. They like to see a management team with complementary business skills, headed by someone who has previous entrepreneurial or profit-and-loss management experience.

Because of their stringent criteria, no more than two to four percent of the ventures contacting venture capital firms receive financing from them. And the equity cost to the entrepreneur can be substantial. Entrepreneurs may give up 35% to 60% or more of the venture's equity for start-up or seed financing, and by the time several rounds of venture financing are complete, they may own no more than 10% to 20% of their company stock.

On the surface, that may not sound very appealing. But it depends on whether your idea and the market opportunity is strong enough to create a very large pie, instead of a small one. Take what may be the most staggering example of all:

Digital Equipment Corporation (DEC), manufacturer of minicomputers, was launched in 1957 by four MIT graduate students, all less than thirty years old. They raised an initial $67,000 of seed capital, giving up 80% of the business to get it. But today their remaining ownership percentage is valued at over $1 billion!

Venture Capital Corporations or Partnerships

There are more than 600 venture capital companies and partnerships in the United States with an established capital base of over $29 billion and managed by 2,000 professionals. Of these about 500 are prviate, independent firms, about 65 are major corporations, and the rest are aligned with banks. Their investment policies cover a range of preferences as to investment size, and the maturity, location, and industry of a venture. Capital for these companies may be provided by one or more wealthy families, one or more financial institutions (e.g., insurance companies, pension funds) and wealthy individuals. Most are organized as limited partnerships, in which the fund managers are the general partners, and the investors the limited partners.

Today, most of these funds prefer to invest upward of $750,000 per round, though some of the smaller funds will go lower. Most of their investments are in the range of $500,000 to $1 million. Some of the so-called "megafunds" with upwards of $100 million and more to invest do not like to consider investments of less than $1 million. One recent study showed the average investment by venture capital firms to be in the $1.5–2 million range. It is noteworthy that among 1500 investments I and my colleague William Bygrave have analyzed, the range was $23,000 to over $50 million! One can see that there are certain dangers in trying to generalize about venture capital.

Their investigation and evaluation of potential investments are thorough and professional. A positive investment decision usually takes from six weeks to eight months after the first meeting with a venture's management. One study reported that the average number of months to get a "yes" was six, while "no" took eleven. Most of their investments are in high-technology businesses. But they will consider investments in most other areas except construction and real estate. In recent years specialized funds have sprung up to invest in specialty retailing, environmental companies and LBOs, for example.

Small Business Investment Companies

SBICs are licensed by the SBA (Small Business Administration) and can obtain from it debt capital—four dollars in loans for each dollar of private equity. An SBIC's equity capital is generally supplied by one or more commercial banks, wealthy individuals and the investing public. There are now about 450 SBICs in the United States, of which about 137 have active venture capital rather than just loan programs; some of these SBICs are affiliates of venture capital firms.

SBICs are limited by law to taking minority shareholder positions and can invest no more than 20% of their equity capital in any one situation. Because SBICs borrow much of their capital from the SBA and must service this debt, they prefer to make some form of interest-bearing investment.

Four common forms of financing are long-term loans with options to buy stock, convertible debentures, straight loans and, in some cases, preferred stock. A typical financing is in the range of $100,000 to $300,000. Also because of their SBA debt, SBICs tend not to finance start-ups and early stage companies but to make investments in more mature companies. SBICs have been an important small business financing source and in over twenty years have invested $3 billion in more than 50,000 businesses.

Corporate Venture Capital

Some nonfinancial corporations (e.g., Monsanto, Emerson Electric, 3M, EG&G) have set up their own venture capital groups. There are currently about 65 that are active. Most corporate venture capitalists are primarily interested in growing their own acquisition candidates. At the time of their initial investment they may arrange to acquire the entrepreneurs' equity at a future time.

Other reasons given for their venture activity are to obtain a "window onto new technologies" (e.g., Digital's investment in Trilogy), and to obtain licenses to manufacture and sell new products. The latter objective was the reason some of the major pharmaceutical companies invested in such biotechnology start-ups as Cetus, which raised $36 million from corporate investors, including Deralb Agresearch and National Distillers in return for rights to use some of the technology from Cetus' genetics research. Notwithstanding this, some corporations (INCO, Analog Devices) have venture capital programs whose objectives are principally capital gains.

From an entrepreneur's point of view, obtaining money from a corporate venture capital group may be a plus, because they have a tendency to overinvest, they are very patient investors with a time horizon of 10 to 20 years for returns, and they have been known to supply $10 million to $20 million.

Strategic Alliances and Corporate Partners

In the 1980s there has been a significant increase in the number of direct investments by larger U. S. and foreign corporations in emerging U. S. companies. One estimate by Venture Economics indicates that this activity had grown from around fifty investments in 1981 to over 300 by 1987. Consider the following example:

An innovator-entrepreneur had raised a small amount of seed capital to develop a prototype for a highly innovative printer-head to compete with existing dot-matrix computer printers. He struck a deal for $1.5 million with a major Japanese company as a strategic partner. The Japanese partner hoped both to utilize the new product in its line of printers and to develop a marketing arrangement with the tiny American firm.

In exchange the small firm may receive any or all of the following: capital market access, equipment, facilities, a technology base, and organizational skills they may not have. What they give up may include equity, additions to the Japanese partner's product line, new opportunities, and knowledge of new applications of the technology.

A strategic alliance offers two possible advantages to the entrepreneur. First, the threshold return on investment may be lower than those of other investment bankers and venture capitalists. Second, the corporate partner can contribute more than money to the fledgling firm. To illustrate:

One of my former students managed to convince a larger firm to become a strategic partner. The larger partner provided $250,000 in advance payments, space in one of their buildings, computers and other equipment, in total equivalent to $600–700,000 in start-up capital. The start-up firm gave up 10%

of the company but kept proprietary rights to the products they sought to develop. Venture capitalists had suggested that they give up 40–45% in return for a similar amount.

The disadvantages of strategic alliances tend to center on four issues. First is the possibility of incompatible and changing goals (particularly if management changes). Second is loss of control and its effect on the entrepreneur's desire for independence. Third, it is often difficult to define or measure success, and the definitions may change, on both sides. Last, how is the relationship resolved? How is a harvest realized by both partners? Often this is not given enough attention up front.

Private Placements

If you are going to sell securities to raise money from a spectrum of sources that range from friends and relatives to wealthy individuals and professional venture capitalists, you must be aware of certain federal and state laws that regulate such fund-raising activities and how such offerings are made.

A new or very young venture will want to avoid having its sale of securities accidentally classified as a "public offering" and being subject to the full gamut of federal securities laws and regulations that govern such issues. Unintentional public offerings because of ignorance of the laws and regulations are potentially very damaging. Disgruntled, unsophisticated stockholders can seek recision of the deal and return of their invested capital. This can result in personal liabilities for a company's management and directors.

How then does a new venture offer securities for its pre-start-up, start-up, and first stage capital and not be subject to the federal regulations governing public offerings?

Because the conditions governing private placements are complex, such offerings of securities should not be undertaken without the advice of an attorney skilled in these matters.

Private placements can be for any amount and involve an offering of stock, subordinated debt or convertible debt, etc. Most private placements for young companies are done under Regulation D of the SEC, which has made the process less complicated than before:

1. For placements less than $500,000, there are no specific disclosure/information requirements, and no limit on the kind or type of purchasers.

2. For security sales over $500,000 and up to $5 million, the criteria for exemption are somewhat more difficult. Sales of securities can be made to an unlimited number of "accredited" purchasers, but not more than 35 "non-accredited" purchasers.

There are no limits on the number or qualifications of the offerees. There are no special information requirements for accredited purchasers. If there are non-accredited as well as accredited purchases, there are specified information disclosure requirements. Investors must also have the opportunity to obtain additional information about the company from its management.

What are accredited and non-accredited investors? Accredited investors include:

- Institutional Investors such as banks, insurance companies, venture capital firms, registered investment companies and SBICs.
- Any person who buys at least $150,000 of the offered security and whose net worth, including that of his or her spouse, is at least five times the purchase price.
- Any person who, together with his or her spouse, has a net worth in excess of $1 million at the time of purchase.
- Any person whose individual income is in excess of $200,000 in each of the last two years, and who expects the same income for the current year.
- Directors, executive officers or general partners of the company or partnership selling the securities.
- Certain tax-exempt organizations with more than $500,000 in assets.
- These are the accredited investors; everyone else is an non-accredited investor.

3. For securities sales in excess of $5 million, the criteria for purchasers is similar: an unlimited number of accredited purchasers, but not more than 35 non-accredited investors. However, the non-accredited

purchasers must be "sophisticated" in investment matters. (Broadly defined, sophisticated investors are wealthy individuals who invest more or less regularly in new and/or early and late stage ventures. They are knowledgeable about the technical and commercial opportunities and risks of the businesses in which they invest. They know what kind of information they want about their prospective investment and have the experience and ability to obtain and analyze the data provided to them.)

There are also specific disclosure requirements which are more detailed than for offerings of up to $5 million. Also, investors must have the opportunity to obtain any additional information from the company and its management.

In addition to meeting the SEC regulations described above, private placements must also comply with the state securities laws in each of the states where the securities will be sold. Registration is simple in some states and more complex in others. Again, the advice of a skilled securities attorney should be obtained for such state registrations.

1244 Stock

Whenever possible, the stock that is issued should be so-called 1244 stock. This stock has a significant tax advantage to investors. Losses from investing in 1244 stock of up to $25,000 (or $50,000 in the case of a joint tax return) can be deducted from ordinary income in any one year, while gains are taxed at the capital gains rate. To be able to issue 1244 stock, a company must have less than $500,000 of capital and paid-in surplus prior to the issue and no more than $1 million in equity after the 1244 offering. Further, a company must have only one class of stock, and receive more than one half its income from sources other than rents and royalties. A 1244 stock-issue plan is adopted by vote of the directors of a company.

Public Stock Offerings

During periods of strong bull markets for new issues, it is possible to raise money for a first-stage and even a start-up from federally registered and underwritten initial pubic offerings (IPOs). There are two main reasons why a new or young company might want to go public. First, in the right times, it will get a higher stock price from an IPO than from venture capital. Second, an IPO establishes a public price for the stock and gives entrepreneurs a sense of wealth—at least on paper, since the sale of their stock will have certain restrictions on it.

A smaller business making a public offering for less than $5 million can use an SEC Form S-18 registration statement instead of the more complex Form S-1. The S-18 offering requires less extensive business and management information than the S-1, and only two years of audited statements rather than three for the S-1. The average costs for an S-18 registration is about two thirds that for an S-1, and the S-18 can be reviewed by the SEC faster than the S-1.

Notwithstanding the rationale for a public offering, and even if a start-up or early stage company could raise money through such a sale of stock, there are a number of reasons why it should not do so.

• A public offering generally costs more than other ways of raising money (private placements, intrastate offerings) for a small young company. The costs of underwriting fees, legal fees, audits, prospectus, etc., can be as high as 15% to 20% for public offerings of $400,000 to $1 million.

• A large amount of management effort, time, and expense are required to comply with SEC (Securities and Exchange Commission) regulations and reporting requirements and to maintain the status of a public company. This diversion of management's time and energy from the tasks of running the company can adversely affect its performance and growth.

• The required disclosures to stockholders and, through them, to outsiders can make known information about a company's products, performance, and financial condition that would be better kept secret.

• The more mature a company is when it makes a public offering, the better the terms of the offering: a higher valuation can be placed on the company and less equity must be given by the founders for the required capital.

• Management can become more interested in maintaining the price of the company's stock and computing their capital gains than in running the company. Short-term activities to maintain or increase this year's earnings can take precedence over longer-term programs to build the company and increase its earnings.

• The liquidity of a company's stock achieved through a public offering may be more apparent than real. Without a sufficient number of shares outstanding and a strong "market maker," there may be no real market for the stock and thus no liquidity.

• The investment banking firms willing to take a new or unseasoned company public may not be the ones with whom you would like to do business and establish a long-term relationship.

How real are these disadvantages? Of about 500 public companies responding to a survey, more than a third said that they would not go public if they had the opportunity to make the decision again, and nearly half said that they had severed their relationship with the underwriter that took them public.

Moreover, of 107 survey respondents that successfully concluded a public offering, nearly all said that the amount of key management time consumed in the underwriting was a moderate to severe problem. Slightly more than half said that unanticipated costs of the underwriting, the amount of disclosure required in the offering prospectus, and the pricing of the issue had been moderate to severe problems. Clearly, the disadvantages and potential problems in a public stock offering are quite real.

In spite of the above, a public offering may, at the right time and under the right circumstances, be the best way for a first-stage or start-up company to raise the money it needs. But this can be true only if a public offering can yield the most net cash for a given amount of equity and if the reasons against a public offering just cited are not serious problems to a company's management. Generally, a company starting up or in its first stage of development would do better to raise its capital via private placements.

8

Approaching Venture Capital Investors

In trying to decide which venture capital firm to contact, an entrepreneur should seek advice and referrals from accountants, lawyers, investment and commercial bankers and business people who are knowledgeable about venture capital. These may be people the entrepreneur knows or can contact through a mutual acquaintance. Especially good sources of information are other entrepreneurs who have recently tried, successfully or unsuccessfully, to raise money for a venture. A good introduction is the best way to gain access. Perhaps 80–90% of the entrepreneurs these investors back are known to them, directly or indirectly.

There are also several directories of venture capital firms that provide basic data on the investment preferences of venture capital firms throughout the U.S. The oldest and most complete of these is the *Guide to Venture Capital Sources,* edited by Stanley Pratt and published by Venture Economics of Needham, Massachusetts (617/431-8100). Also available from Venture Economics is a computerized data base of over 500 venture capital firms which can be searched to identify the most likely prospects for your venture.

It is a good idea to review the list with other entrepreneurs or outside professionals who can help you narrow the search. From such sources, the entrepreneur should determine the appetite of target investors for ventures of the age, industry, technology and capital requirements proposed by the entrepreneurs. It is also desirable to determine which venture capital firms have money to invest, are actively seeking deals and have the time and people to investigate new deals. If the fund was formed recently, up to two or three years ago, it will be in an active investing mode. Part of your research will also reveal the size of investments the fund prefers, whether it will do start-up and early stage deals, or prefers downstream expansion financings or LBOs and MBOs. If entrepreneurs don't screen prospective venture capital firms, they will waste time and effort trying to raise money.

Contacting Venture Capital Firms

Having identified venture capitalists who might be interested in his or her venture, the entrepreneur must not approach such a large number of them that the venture becomes shopworn in the close-knit venture capital community. Regardless of the merits of a particular venture, this will discourage many venture capitalists from making an investment. They don't like to invest in a situation that has been turned down by many others in the field. If they go ahead and invest when others have said "no thanks" and the deal turns sour, they look pretty dumb. Consequently, early rejections can haunt you.

How can this be avoided? An entrepreneur does want to expose the deal to more than one potential investor—this is no more than good business practice. However, mass mailing a business plan to a large number of venture capital investors is not the thing to do. The best way for entrepreneurs to proceed is to identify and contact a small number (five to ten) of investors who have a reasonable probability of being interested in the entrepreneurs' venture. In the cellular phone company example noted earlier , we identified what we believed to be the six best potential financial partners in the country. Five were clearly interested. Two of them we were enthusiastic about, although any of the five would been acceptable.

To receive the proper attention from potential investors, it is desirable that entrepreneurs be properly introduced to them. This can be done by a lawyer, banker, or another entrepreneur who may have suggested a particular investor to the entre-preneur. Or, if they are uncomfortable doing this, by someone else that they know who knows the investor. This referral need not be much more than a telephone call to the investor to tell him that a particular entrepreneur and venture are worthy of his consideration.

Some entrepreneurs who are having difficulty obtaining such introductions often consider employing a finder, or intermediary. These people will introduce them to potential investors and, if an introduction results in an investment, receive a fee—up to five percent of larger deals, and as much as ten percent of smaller ones. There are some good, effective finders around; the problem is in knowing who they are. You should also know that some venture capital investors don't like finders or paying finder's fees. One bit of advice: unless your state has—as does Massachusetts—a law which requires a written agreement in order for the finder to collect a fee, you are exposed to unscrupulous people who may show up just prior to the closing and insist on a fee (read blackmail) even though you had only a casual phone conversation months earlier.

With or without a referral, an entrepreneur's initial contact with a potential investor will usually be via a telephone call. During this first contact, the entrepreneur will describe his or her venture, its products, the backgrounds of its management team, the amount of capital sought and the expected performance of the venture two or three years after the investment is made. The entrepreneur must convey enough of the potential of the venture to persuade the investor to find out more about it.

On the other side, the venture capital investor is making a quick evaluation of the entrepreneur's venture to determine if it is worth asking the entrepreneur to submit a business plan or, perhaps, make a presentation. Generally, the investor will request to see a business plan before agreeing to meet with an entrepreneur.

Somewhere between 60% and 80% of all ventures presented to a venture capitalist are rejected during this first telephone contact. Venture capitalists will agree to go a next step and review a business plan only if they believe the entrepreneur and his team appear to have the relevant experience and the required management skills, and if the venture's product fulfills a need in a large and growing market. Avoid giving the impression that yours is a unique product creating a market. It is much better to describe a product as a response to a clearly identified market need.

An entrepreneur should not be discouraged by a rejection at this point. The investor may not like the industry of the venture, may have too many investments in that industry, or have some other reason for the rejection that is unrelated to the quality of the entrepreneur and the venture. On the other hand, the entrepreneur may have done a poor job presenting the venture, or the investor may perceive some flaw in the venture.

In any case, if a venture is rejected, the entrepreneur should review the basic data about the venture and the way the venture is presented to an investor. A majority (70%) of "rejects" manage to carry on and are in business three years later. Even if you have faced numerous rejections, there may be an alternative way to identify prospects, if you have not already done so. Consider the following:

I suggested to an entrepreneur who had faced similar rejections that he identify the investors around the nation who had already invested in some of his potential customers, in this case the semiconductor industry. After nearly eighteen months of getting nowhere, he was able to raise financing in two to three months. As we expected, they were ideal investors, who quickly grasped and appreciated the value added and market potential of his novel and very sophisticated technology.

Investor Screening of the Business Plan

Those entrepreneurs and ventures that pass the initial telephone contact are asked to submit their business plans to the investor. On the basis of a quick screening of the business plans (one hour or less) and perhaps another telephone call to clarify a point, the venture capital investors will decide whether or not a venture receives further consideration. This investor screening process focuses on:

• *The caliber of the management team.* Do they have a successful track record? Do the experience, know-how and skills of the principals seem to be up to the job of developing a growth business? Has the president had profit and loss responsibility, and are the results impressive? Has the team worked together and built a division or another business? Is their experience highly relevant to the technology, market, distribution and manufacturing know-how necessary to be a winner in this industry?

• *The industry and technology of the venture.* Is the venture in an industry that the investor understands and has previously invested in successfully? Is the venture in a growth and glamour industry?

• *Uniqueness of the venture.* Does the venture have a unique or really superior product, technology or skill that can give it a significant proprietary or other competitive advantage?

• *Financial data.* If an existing venture, does it have a positive net worth and working capital? Is the venture borrowed to capacity? Are there any questionable or troublesome assets (overcapitalized patents) or liabilities (unpaid and deferred withholding taxes)? Are the magnitudes of current and projected sales and profits high enough to be interesting?

• *Terms of the deal.* How much equity is being offered for how much money? Is the ratio reasonable or unreasonable?

If, in the screening of the business plan, the investor finds no fatal flaws in the above areas that would be cause for rejecting the venture, the entrepreneur will be asked to make an oral presentation to the investor and his or her associates. At this point, no more than 10% to 20% of all the entrepreneurs who originally contacted the investor are still being considered.

The Quest for the "Golden Ring"

The investor's search for the elusive "golden ring"[1] is the search for the "super deal." While such ventures are few and far between (less than 10% of all investments made by venture capitalists ever achieve such objectives) these characteristics are invariably sought. The table below summarizes the criteria most investors get excited about.

Characteristics of the "Super Deal" (Investor's perspective)

Mission
- Build a highly profitable and industry-dominant company.
- Go public or merge within 4–7 years at a high price/earnings multiple.

Management Team
- Complete team, led by industry superstar.
- Proven entrepreneurial, general management and P&L experience in the business.
- Leading innovator or technologist and marketing head.

1 A thorough treatment of what constitutes a good new business opportunity, versus just another idea, is focus of one of my other books, *New Business Opportunities* (1989, Brick House Publishing Co., Acton MA).

- Complementary and compatible skills.
- Unusual tenacity, imagination and commitment.
- Reputation for high degree of integrity.

Proprietary Product
- Significant competitive lead and "unfair" advantages.
- High value-added properties resulting in early payback to user.
- Can gain exclusive contractual or legal rights.

Rapid Market Growth
- No dominant competitor now.
- Market currently at $100 million and growing 25% plus per year.
- Will accommodate $50 million entrant in five years.
- Clearly identified customers and distribution channels.

Forgiving and Rewarding Economics
- Positive cash flow and breakeven sales achievable early.
- Gross margins of 40–50% or more.
- 10% plus profit after tax.

Deal Valuation and ROR
- Digestible first-round capital requirements (over $1 million, less than $10 million).
- Ten times original investment in five years, at P/E of fifteen plus.
- Additional rounds of financing at substantial mark-up.
- Anti-dilution and initial public offering subscription rights.

Presentation to the Investor

The oral presentation is an important milestone in the raising of capital from an investor. It is usually the first, and if handled improperly the only face-to-face opportunity entrepreneurs have to convince an investor. The entrepreneur and one to three key members of his or her management team should prepare for and make the presentation. Each individual describes and discusses that part of the business for which he or she will be responsible.

The presentation is usually made at the venture capitalist's office in the case of start-ups and early-stage ventures. In the case of a going venture, the meeting is more likely to occur at the venture's facilities. It can take anywhere from two or three days to two weeks from the time of telephone contact to this meeting.

It should be rehearsed. Avoid a slick, high-pressure "dog and pony show." Show confidence, not arrogance, by selling the "steak," not the "sizzle." Key facts, figures and other knowledge should be in your head, thereby avoiding frequent dives into file folders.

The presentation should highlight and discuss the key material in the business plan. Particular stress should be placed on:

• analysis of the opportunity and market for the venture's products and why those products can establish a market niche against their competition.

• the unique skills and backgrounds of the key members of the management team that qualify them for their role in the venture, and how it will be built as the venture grows.

• discussion of the history of the venture, as appropriate.

• a brief view of projected sales and profits and the key assumptions.

• recognition and discussion of potential risks and problems, showing you have the ability to think through the tough trade-offs and devise alternate action plans.

• recognition that the investors are quite busy and need a short summary of your team and plan.

• a succinct list of who owns what shares in the company and who has paid what.

• a summary of the details of your proposed deal, the price, shares or range.

It's not a bad idea to bring along prototype product brochures, videos or slides and to use flip charts for presenting key materials.

Venture capital investors are interested in the presentation not only for what they will learn about the venture, but also for the opportunity to meet the entrepreneur and management team, to judge their individual capabilities and their ability to function as an effective team.

Some or all of the investors present will have read the entrepreneur's business proposal. They will have some hard questions to ask. They will be interested in not only the answers, but who answers them, and how they are answered. They will be looking for evidence of business knowledge and experience in specific areas of the venture (marketing, finance, etc.) that are of concern to them.

If a venture's marketing manager, for example, is unable to provide answers that indicate an understanding of the size and growth of the venture's market and the competition, or cannot explain the rationale for a particular sales strategy, the investor may have serious questions about that manager's capability and about the venture itself.

A good illustration of what the entrepreneur should not do in handling the financial questions happened a few years ago. I was working in Alaska helping the Alaska Renewable Resources Corporation in their efforts to invest their funds in the state. The owner of a good salmon cannery was due for a discussion of her business plan and financing needs for a debt-ridden, marginally performing business. She showed up in a full-length, elegant mink coat, and brought along her acountant. Questions immediately focused on the cash-flow situation, breakeven and implications for additional capital.

Two fatal mistakes followed. First, she claimed basic ignorance of financial matters—a serious flaw in the owner-president of a struggling multi-million-dollar business—and deferred all questions to her accountant. Second, she had clearly brought the wrong accountant. He was prepared to talk about the accrual-based financial statements of the prior year—ancient history from our perspective, and useless in trying to get a clear understanding of present and projected cash flow, breakeven and capital requirements.

Similarly, a tendency for the entrepreneur to bypass his management team and answer all questions can raise doubts about the capabilities of the management team and the entrepreneur's ability to be an effective leader. Any attempt by the entrepreneur to dodge tough questions, ignore or be ignorant of risks and problems, or "know all the answers" will be viewed unfavorably by the investors. Likewise, be very careful not to say anything that would be the slightest misrepresentation of your past or to the results you claim. Investors check thoroughly and any falsehoods, suspected or real, are the kiss of death.

Over the years, the best entrepreneurs I have known and worked with are savvy about what they do and don't know. They have a voracious appetite for finding out and compensating for any blind spots.

After the initial meeting and presentation, the venture capitalist will decide either to reject the venture or to go ahead with a serious investigation of the venture and its management. This action should not be viewed as a positive decision but, rather, the absence of a negative decision. While a venture capitalist is checking out a venture (known as "due diligence"), the entrepreneur can also check out the investor, and should definitely do so.

The entrepreneur should also discreetly make presentations to a limited number of other venture capitalists, some of whom may be suggested by the interested investor. There are several reasons for doing this. First, if entrepreneurs do not do it, they may find themselves turned down after two to three months, short on cash and in a poor bargaining position with investors they approach later. Second, exposure to more than one venture capitalist is desirable if entrepreneurs are to learn how attractive and worthwhile are their ventures. Last, if the venture requires financing that exceeds the limit of one venture firm, other investors will have to be brought into the deal and will want presentations. Further, many times venture firms like to involve other venture investors so that there are enough "deep pockets" to provide some or all of the capital for subsequent financings.

Notwithstanding this advice, once a venture capitalist commits to finance a venture and the offer is accepted through execution of the "terms sheet," the entrepreneur faces a delicate situation. He may have agreed to a deal, but unless and until the money is in the bank, the hard truth is that the deal is not closed. One effective way to handle this is to make it perfectly clear that you do not consider the deal done until then. The first investor who produces a check will be your partner, otherwise you do not have a deal.

It is fair to argue that you have a responsibility to all of your other constituencies—partners, family, employees, customers, vendors, etc.—to have other live alternatives. If you abandon all other alternatives, you accept a non-trivial risk of going through several weeks of negotiations, running out of cash, and ending up at a disadvantage in negotiating final details. What is worse, the devil is in the details, not the terms sheet. The best possible way to keep investors fair and realistic in all aspects of the final negotiations is simply to have alternative sources of financing.

Investigation of a Venture

The investigation and analysis of a business by venture capitalists are extensive. The process includes checks on management, the markets for the product, technical feasibility and detailed financial analysis. Typically, an investigation takes six to ten weeks. Start-ups take longer to assess than later-stage ventures. It might require three to six months to obtain a "yes," and often up to a year to get a final "no."

Venture capitalists agree that the entrepreneur and his management team are the most important factors in the success and growth of a business. Accordingly, much of their evaluation of a business involves getting to know the entrepreneur and the team in depth and observing how they perform in a variety of situations and under stress.

These situations can involve requests for more data regarding the venture's market or competitors, or meetings and discussions with the entrepreneurial team to probe various aspects of the business (financing, future performance, risks, etc.) as well as the skills, attitudes, motivations, and commitment of the entrepreneur and the team.

The venture capitalist also has conversations with former employers, business associates, bankers, and technical references to check out the business records and competence of the entrepreneur and his key associates. A credit check is often conducted to make sure there is nothing dishonest or disreputable about the entrepreneur and the other venture principals.

As part of their investigations, venture capitalists verify the claims and data about the venture's technology, products, markets, and industry trends. This may be done by talking to such people as the entrepreneur's suppliers, customers, competitors, customers of competitors, and knowledgeable business and technical acquaintances of the venture capitalists in the venture's industry.

In many cases venture capitalists use a technical consultant for a market appraisal or to evaluate the technical feasibility of a venture's product. Trade association and industry statistics are examined to verify market trends, and competitors' track records may be studied to obtain an indication of the venture's growth, profitability and harvest potential.

Only about one to three percent of all ventures seen by venture capital investors make it past the final evaluation to a positive decision and investment.

Dealing with Rejection

Because such a small percentage of the ventures seeking an investment from the venture capital community obtain it, most entrepreneurs will get more than one rejection in seeking such financing. Good entrepreneurs are persistent, and most will continue for up to a year to seek financing in the face of a number of rejections, and in some unusual cases for nearly three years.

Some entrepreneurs keep trying even longer, and eventually obtain financing and go on to build a successful company. Others do not, and the financial and psychic costs of a fruitless search for investors can be substantial, especially if an entrepreneur has quit a job to avoid conflicts with an employer and to have more time available for fund-raising.

To avoid this sort of experience, entrepreneurs should try to discover the true reason for a rejection. This is not easy. Most venture capitalists will reject a venture by saying, "Interesting venture, but it does not meet our investment criteria," or "Interesting deal and good management. But we are not lead investors. If you find a strong lead investor, we might be very interested."

These are polite ways of saying no. If an entrepreneur is to avoid wasting time and money, and perhaps turn a rejection into an acceptance, he or she must get an investor to explain the true reason for a rejection. When this is done, the entrepreneur can either correct the flaw in the venture (e.g., obtain an experienced marketing manager) or decide the venture has basic limitations (e.g., a small market for its products) which make obtaining venture capital improbable if not impossible.

When all is said and done, as one research project showed, fully 70% of all such rejects were still in business three years later.

9

Sources of Debt Capital: Trade Credit and Commercial Banks

The principal sources of borrowed capital for new and young businesses are trade credit, commercial banks, finance companies, factors, and leasing companies. Admittedly, start-ups have more difficulty borrowing money than existing businesses. Nevertheless, start-ups managed by an entrepreneur with a track record, with significant equity in the business and who can present a sound business plan can borrow money from one or more sources. But if little equity or collateral exists, the start-up won't have much success with banks.

The availability of such debt depends, in part, on where the business is located. In such hotbeds of entrepreneurial activity as Eastern Massachusetts and Silicon Valley in California, debt and leases as well as equity capital are more available to start-up companies than, say, in the midwest. Also, in the hotbed areas there is close contact between venture capital firms and the high-technology lending officers of banks. This contact tends to make it easier for start-ups and early stage companies to borrow money.

Trade Credit

Trade credit is a major source of short-term funds for the small business. In fact, trade credit represents 30% to 40% of the current liabilities of non-financial businesses, with generally higher percentages in small companies. Trade credit is reflected on the balance sheet as accounts payable.

If a small business is able to buy goods and services and be given, or take, 30, 60, or 90 days to pay for them, that business has essentially obtained a loan of 30 to 90 days. Many small and new businesses are able to obtain such trade credit when no other form of debt financing is available to them. Suppliers offer such trade credit as a way of getting new customers, and often build the "bad debt" risk into their prices.

The ability of a new business to obtain trade credit depends on the quality and reputation of its management and the relationships it establishes with its suppliers. A word of warning: continued late or non-payment may cause suppliers to cut off shipments, or ship only on a C.O.D. basis. Also, the real cost of using trade credit can be very high, for example, the loss of discounts for prompt payment. Because the cost of trade credit is seldom expressed as an annual amount, it should be analyzed carefully, and a new business should shop for the best terms.

Some of the forms that trade credit may take are extended credit terms; special or seasonal datings, where a supplier ships goods in advance of the purchaser's peak selling season and accepts payment 90 or 120 days later during the season; inventory on consignment, not requiring payment until sold; and loan or lease of equipment.

Commercial Bank Financing

Commercial banks prefer to lend to existing business who have a track record of sales, profits and satisfied customers and a current backlog. Their concern about the high failure rates in new businesses can make them less than enthusiastic about making loans to such firms. They like to be no-risk lenders. For their protection, they look first to positive cash flow, and then to collateral, and in new and young businesses they are likely to require personal guarantees of the owners' business. Like equity investors, they place great weight on the quality of the management team.

Notwithstanding this, banks do make loans to start-ups or young businesses that have strong equity financing from venture capital firms. This is especially true in such centers of entre-preneurial and venture capital activity as Silicon Valley, Boston, and Los Angeles.

Commercial banks are the primary source of debt capital for existing (not new) small and medium-sized businesses, those with less than $5 million in sales. Small business loans may be handled by a bank's small business loan department. Larger loans may require the approval of a loan committee. If a loan exceeds the limits of a local bank, part or all of the loan will be offered to "correspondent" banks in neighboring communities and nearby financial centers. This correspondent network enables the smaller banks in rural areas to handle loans that otherwise could not be made.

Most of the loans made by commercial banks are for one year or less. Some of these loans are unsecured and others are secured by receivables, inventories, or other assets. Commercial banks also make a large number of intermediate-term loans (or "term loans") with a maturity of one to five years. On about 90% of these term loans, the banks require collateral, generally consisting of stocks, machinery, equipment, and real estate. Most term loans are retired by systematic payments over the life of the loan. Apart from real-estate mortgages and loans guaranteed by the SBA or a similar organization, commercial banks make few loans with maturities greater than five years.

Banks also offer a number of services to the small business, such as computerized payroll preparation, letters of credit, international services, lease financing and money market accounts.

There are almost 14,000 commercial banks in the United States. A complete listing of these banks can be found, arranged by state, in the American Bank Directory (McFadden Business Publications), published semiannually.

Line of Credit Loans

A line of credit is a formal or informal agreement between a bank and borrower concerning the maximum loan balance a bank will allow the borrower for a one-year period. Often the bank will charge a fee of some percent of the line of credit for a definite commitment to make the loan when requested.

Line of credit funds are used for such seasonal financings as inventory build-up and receivable financing. It is general practice to repay these loans from the sales and liquidation of short-term assets that they financed. Lines of credit can be unsecured, but often a bank will require a pledge of inventory, receivables, equipment, or other acceptable assets. Unsecured lines of credit have no lien on any asset of the borrower and no priority over any trade creditor, but the banks do require that all debt to the principals and stockholders of the company be subordinated to line of credit debt.

The line of credit is executed through a series of renewable ninety-day notes or through an installment loan to be paid up within the year. The renewable ninety-day note is the more common practice, and the bank will expect the borrower to pay off his open line within a year and hold a zero loan balance for one to two months. This is known as "resting the line." Commercial banks may also generally require that a borrower maintain a checking account at the bank with a minimum or "compensating" balance of 15% to 20% of the outstanding loan.

For a large, financially sound company, the interest rates for a "prime risk" line of credit will be quoted at about one to two percent over the rediscount rate charged by the Federal Reserve. A small firm may be required to pay a higher rate. It should be noted that the true rate of interest will depend on the method of charging interest. If the bank deducts interest in advance (discounts the loan) or the loan is repaid in installments, the effective rate of interest will be higher than the quoted figure. Any "compensating balance" or "resting the line" requirements will also increase effective interest rates.

Accounts Receivable Financing

Accounts receivable financing is short-term financing that involves either the pledge of receivables as collateral for a loan or the sale of receivables (factoring). Accounts receivable loans are made by commercial banks, whereas factoring is done primarily by commercial finance companies and factoring concerns. Only a very limited number of banks do factoring.

Accounts receivable bank loans are made on a discounted value of the receivables pledged. Invoices that do not meet the bank's credit standard will not be accepted as collateral. (Receivables more than ninety days old are not normally accepted.) A bank may inform the purchaser of goods that his account has been assigned to the bank. Payments are made directly to the bank, which credits them to the borrower's account. This is called a "notification" plan. Alternatively, the borrower collects his accounts as usual and pays off his bank loan. This is a "non-notification" plan.

Accounts receivable loans can make it possible for a company to secure a loan that it might not otherwise get. The loan can be increased as sales and receivables grow. However, receivables loans do have drawbacks. They can be expensive, and receivable financing is sometimes regarded by trade creditors as evidence of a company in financial difficulty.

Time-Sales Finance

Many dealers or manufacturers who offer installment payment terms to purchasers of their equipment cannot, themselves, finance installment or conditional sales contracts. In such situations, they sell and assign the installment contract to a bank or sales finance company. (Some very large manufacturers do their own financing through captive finance companies; most very small retailers merely refer their customers to consumer finance companies.) Although commercial banks are becoming more active in the financing of commercial and consumer installment contracts, sales finance companies provide more of this financing, and on more flexible terms.

From the manufacturer's or dealer's point of view, time-sales finance is, in effect, a way of obtaining short-term financing from long-term installment accounts receivable. From the purchaser's point of view, it is a way of financing the purchase of new equipment.

Under time-sales financing, the bank purchases installment contracts at a discount from their full value and takes as security an assignment of the manufacturer/dealer's interest in the conditional sales contract. In addition, the bank's financing of installment note receivables includes recourse to the seller in the event of loan default by the purchaser. Thus the bank has the payment obligation of the equipment purchaser, the manufacturer/dealer's security interest in the equipment purchased, and recourse to the manufacturer/dealer in the event of default. The bank also withholds a portion of the payment (five percent or more) as a dealer reserve until the note is paid. Since the reserve becomes an increasing percentage of the note as the contract is paid off, an arrangement is often made when multiple contracts are financed to insure that the reserve against all contracts will not exceed 20% or so.

The purchase price of equipment under a sales financing arrangement includes a "time-sales price differential"—e.g., an increase to cover the discount (typically six to ten percent) taken by the bank that does the financing. Collection of the installments may be made directly by the bank or indirectly through the manufacturer/dealer.

Unsecured Term Loans

Bank term loans are generally made for periods of from one to five years, and may be unsecured or secured. Most of the basic features of bank term loans are the same for secured and unsecured loans. Secured term loans are described below under chattel mortgages and collateral loans.

Term loans provide needed growth capital to companies that could not obtain such capital from the sale of stock. They are also a substitute for a series of short-term loans made with the anticipation of renewal by both the borrower and the lender.

Term loans have three distinguishing features: They are made by banks for periods of up to five years (and occasionally more). Periodic repayment is required. Term loan agreements are designed to fit the special needs and requirements of the borrower; e.g., payments can be smaller at the beginning of a loan term and larger at the end.

Because term loans do not mature for a number of years, during which time there could be a significant change in the situation and fortunes of the borrower, the bank must carefully evaluate the prospects and management of the borrowing company. Even the protection afforded by initially strong assets can be wiped out by several years of heavy losses. Term lenders place particular stress on the entrepreneurial and managerial abilities of the borrowing company. The bank will also carefully consider such things as the long-range prospects of the company and its industry, its present and projected profitability, and its ability to generate the cash required to meet the loan payments.

To lessen the risks involved in term loans, a bank will require some restrictive covenants in the loan agreement. These covenants might prohibit additional borrowing, merger of the company, payment of dividends, sales of assets, etc.

Chattel Mortgages and Equipment Loans

Assigning an appropriate possession (chattel) as security is a common way of making secured term loans. The chattel is any machinery, equipment, or business property that is made the collateral of a loan in the same way as a mortgage on real estate. The chattel remains with the borrower unless there is default, in which case the chattel goes to the bank. Generally, credit against machinery and equipment is restricted primarily to new or highly serviceable and salable used items.

It should be noted that in many states, loans that used to be chattel mortgages are now executed through the security agreement forms of the Uniform Commercial Code (UCC). However, chattel mortgages are still used in many places and, from custom, many lenders continue to use that term even though the loans are executed through the UCC's security agreements. The term of chattel mortgages is typically from one to five years; some are longer term.

Conditional Sales Contracts

Conditional sales contracts are used to finance a substantial portion of the new equipment purchased by businesses. Under a sales contract, the buyer agrees to purchase a piece of equipment, makes a nominal down payment, and pays the balance in installments over a period of from one to five years. Until payment is complete, the seller holds title to the equipment. Hence, the sale is conditional upon the buyer's completing the payments.

A sales contract is financed by a bank that has recourse to the seller, should the purchaser default the loan. This makes it easier to finance a new piece of equipment from a machinery dealer than to finance the purchase of a good piece of used equipment at an auction. No recourse to the seller is available if the equipment is purchased at an auction; the bank would have to sell the equipment if the loan goes bad. Occasionally, a firm seeking financing on existing and new equipment will sell some of its equipment to a dealer and repurchase it, together with new equipment, in order to get a conditional sales contract financed by a bank.

The effective rate of interest on a conditional sales contract is high, running to as much as 15% to 18% if the effect of installment features is considered. The purchaser/borrower should thus make sure that the interest payment is covered by increased productivity and profitability resulting from the new equipment.

Plant Improvement Loans

Loans made to finance improvements to business properties and plants are called plant improvement loans. They can be intermediate- or long-term and are generally secured by a first mortgage on that part of the property or plant which is being improved.

How to Borrow Money: The Loan Package

In Chapter 11 I cover in detail the bank's perspective, how to be prepared with a convincing loan package, and other key issues in finding and working with the right bank and banker. Personal guarantees of loans and how to avoid them will also be covered.

10

Sources of Debt Capital: Finance, Factor and Leasing Companies

Commercial Finance Companies

The commercial bank is generally the lender of choice for a business. From whom does a business seek loans when the bank says no? Commercial finance companies, who aggressively seek borrowers. They frequently loan money to companies that do not have positive cash flow—although they will not make loans to companies unless they consider them viable.

The primary factor in a bank's loan decision is the continuing successful operation of a business, and its generation of more than enough cash to repay a loan. Commercial finance companies lend against the liquidation value of assets (receivables, inventory, equipment) that it understands, knows how and where to sell, and whose liquidation value is sufficient to repay the loan.

In the case of inventories or equipment, liquidation value is the amount that could be realized from an auction or quick sale. Finance companies will generally *not* lend against receivables more than 90 days old, federal or state government agency receivables (because they are slow payers) or any receivables whose collection is contingent on the performance of a delivered product.

Because of the liquidation criteria, finance companies prefer readily salable inventory items such as electronic components, or metal in such commodity forms as billets or standard shapes. Generally, a finance company will not accept inventory as collateral unless it also has receivables. As for equipment loans, these are made only by certain finance companies and against such standard equipment as lathes, milling machines, etc.

How much of the value of collateral will a finance company lend? Generally 70% to 80% of acceptable receivables under 90 days old, 42% to 50% of the liquidation value of raw materials and/or finished goods inventory that aren't obsolete or damaged, and 60% to 70% of the liquidation value of equipment, as determined by an appraiser. Receivables and inventory loans are for one year, while equipment loans are for three to seven years.

All of these loans have tough prepayment penalties: finance companies don't want to be immediately replaced by banks when a borrower has improved its credit image.

The data required for a loan from a finance company includes all that would be provided to a bank, plus additional details of the assets being used as collateral. For receivables financing this includes detailed aging of receivables (and payables) and historical data on sales, returns and collections (see Chapter 11).

For inventory financing, it includes details on the items in inventory, how long they have been there and their rate of turnover. Requests for equipment loans should be accompanied by details on the date of purchase, cost of each equipment item and appraisals, if available. If not, the finance company will have such an appraisal made.

The advantage of dealing with a commercial finance company is that it will make loans that banks will not, and it can be flexible in lending arrangements. The price a finance company exacts for this is an interest rate anywhere from two to six percent over that charged by a bank, prepayment penalties and, in the case of receivables loans, recourse to the borrower for unpaid collateralized receivables.

Because of their greater risk-taking and asset-based lending, finance companies usually place a larger reporting and monitoring burden on the borrowing firm in order to stay on top of the receivables and inventory serving as loan collateral. Personal guarantees will generally be required from the principals of a business. The finance company will generally reserve the right to reduce the percentage of value lent against receivables or inventory if it gets nervous about the borrower's survivability.

Factoring

Factoring is a form of accounts receivable financing. However, instead of borrowing and using receivables as collateral, the receivables are sold, at a discounted value, to a factor. Some commercial finance companies do factoring. The factor provides receivables financing for the company unable to obtain such financing from a bank.

In a standard factoring arrangement, the factor buys the client's receivables outright, without recourse, as soon as the client creates them by its shipment of goods to customers. Although the factor has recourse to the borrower for returns, errors in pricing, etc., the factor assumes the risk of bad debt losses that develop from receivables it approves and purchases.

Cash is made available to the client as soon as proof of shipment is provided (old-line factoring) or on the average due date of the invoices (maturity factoring). With maturity factoring, the company can often obtain a loan of about 90% of the money a factor has agreed pay to him on the maturity date. Most factoring arrangements are for one year.

Factoring fits some businesses better than others. For a business has an annual sales volume in excess of $300,000, a net worth over $50,000 and sells on normal credit terms to a customer base that is 75% credit rated, factoring is a real option. Factoring has become almost traditional in such industries as textiles, furniture manufacturing, clothing manufacturing, toys, shoes and plastics.

The same data required from a business for a receivable loan from a bank is required by a factor. Because a factor is buying receivables with no recourse, it will analyze carefully the quality and value of a prospective client's receivables. It will want a detailed aging of receivables plus historical data on bad debts, returns and allowances. It will also investigate the credit history of customers to whom its client sells, and establish credit limits for each customer. The business client can receive factoring of customer receivables only up to the limits so set.

The cost of financing receivables through factoring is higher than that of borrowing from a bank or a finance company. The factor is assuming the credit risk, doing credit investigations and collections, and advancing funds. A factor generally charges up to two percent of the total sales factored as a service charge.

There is also an interest charge for money advanced to a business, usually two to six percent above prime. A larger, established business borrowing large sums will command a better interest rate than the small borrower with a one-time, short-term need. Finally, factors withhold a reserve of five to ten percent of the receivables purchased.

Factoring is not the cheapest way to obtain capital, but it does quickly turn receivables into cash. Moreover, although more expensive than accounts receivable financing, factoring saves its users credit agency fees, salaries of credit and collection personnel, and bad debt write-offs.

Leasing Companies

The leasing industry has grown substantially in recent years, and lease financing has become an important source of medium-term financing for businesses. There are about 700 to 800 leasing companies in the United States. In addition, many commercial banks and finance companies have leasing departments. Some leasing companies handle a wide variety of equipment, while others specialize in certain types of equipment—machine tools, electronic test equipment, etc.

Common and readily resalable items such as automobiles and trucks, typewriters and office furniture can be leased by both new and existing businesses. However, the start-up will find it difficult to lease other kinds of industrial, computer or business equipment without providing a certificate of deposit to secure the lease or personal guarantees from the founders or from a wealthy third party.

An exception to this are high-technology start-ups that have received substantial venture capital. Some of these ventures have received large amounts of lease financing for rather special equipment from equity-oriented lessors, who receive some form of stock purchase rights in return for providing the start-up's lease line. Two companies doing this sort of venture leasing are Equitec of Oakland, California, with offices in Boston, New York and Dallas, and Intertec of Mill Valley, California.

Generally, industrial equipment leases have a term of three to five years, but in some cases may run longer. There can also be lease renewal options for three to five percent per year of the original equipment value. Leases are usually structured to return the entire cost of the leased equipment plus finance charges to the lessor, although some so-called operating leases do not, over their term, produce revenues equal or greater than the price of the leased equipment.

Typically, an up-front payment is required of about 10% of the value of the item being leased. The interest rate on equipment leasing may be more or less than other forms of financing depending on the equipment leased, the credit of the lessee and the time of the year.

Leasing credit criteria are very similar to the criteria used by commercial banks for equipment loans. Primary considerations are the value of the equipment leased, the justification of the lease, and the lessee's projected cash flow over the lease term.

Should a business lease equipment? Leasing has certain advantages. It enables a young or growing company to conserve cash, and can reduce its requirements for equity capital. Leasing can also be a tax advantage, because payments can be deducted over a shorter period than depreciation.

Finally, leasing provides the flexibility of returning equip-ment after the lease period if it is no longer needed or if it has become technologically obsolete. This can be a particular ad-vantage to companies in high technology industries.

Leasing no longer improves a company's balance sheet, because accounting practice now requires that the value of the equipment leased be capitalized and a lease liability shown.

11

Borrowing Capital:
Before the Loan Decision

Choosing a bank and, more specifically, a banker, is one of the more important decisions that a new or young business will make. A good lender relationship can sometimes mean the difference between the life and death of a business during difficult times. There have been cases where, other things being equal, one bank has called its loans to a struggling business, causing it to go under, and another bank has stayed with its loans and helped a business to survive and prosper. (Although I refer specifically to banks and banking relationships, much of what follows on lending practices and decisions applies as well to commercial finance company lenders.)

Some banks and bankers will make loans to start-ups and early-stage ventures and others will not. Those that will not generally cite the lack of an operating "track record" as the reason for turning down the loan. Lenders that make such loans usually do so for previously successful entrepreneurs of means or for firms backed by investors with whom they had prior relationships and whose judgment they trust—established venture capital firms, for example.

In centers of high technology and venture capital the main officers of major banks will have one or more high-technology lending officers who specialize in making loans to early-stage high-technology ventures. Through much experience, these bankers have come to understand the market and operating idiosyncrasies, problems and opportunities of such ventures. They generally have close ties to venture capital firms and will refer entrepreneurs to such firms for possible equity financing. The venture capital firms, in turn, will refer their portfolio ventures to the banker for debt financing.

What should an entrepreneur consider in choosing a lender? What is important in a lending decision? How should entrepreneurs relate to their lenders on an ongoing basis? In many ways, the lender's decision process is similar to that of the venture capitalist. His goal is to make money for his company, through interest earned on good loans. He fears losing money by making bad loans to companies that default on their loans. To this end, he avoids risk by building in every safeguard he can think of. He is concerned with the client company's loan coverage: its ability to repay and the collateral it can offer. Finally, but most important, he must judge the character and quality of the key managers of the company to whom he is making the loan.

Key Steps in Obtaining a Loan

Before choosing and approaching a banker or other lender, the entrepreneur and his management team should go through the following steps in preparing to ask for a loan.

- Decide how much growth they want, and how fast they want to grow, observing the dictum that financing *follows* strategy.
- Determine how much money they require, and when they need to have it. To this end, they must
    - develop a schedule of operating and asset needs,
    - prepare a real-time cash-flow projection;
    - decide how much capital they need,
    - specify how they will use the funds they borrow.
- Revise and update the "corporate profile" in their business plan. This should consist of
    - the core ingredients of the plan in the form of an executive summary,
    - a history of the firm (as appropriate),
    - summaries of the financial results of the past three years,
    - succinct descriptions of their markets and products,
    - a description of their operations,
    - statements of cash flow and financial requirements,
    - descriptions of the key managers, owners and directors,
    - a rundown of the key strategies, facts and logic that guides them in growing their corporation.
- Identify potential sources for the type of debt they seek, and the *amount, rate, terms and conditions* they seek.
- Select a bank or other lending institution, solicit interest and prepare a presentation.

- Prepare a *written loan request.*
- Present their case, negotiate and then close the deal.
- After the loan is granted, it is important that the borrowers maintain an effective relationship with the lending officer.

Choosing a Banker

Because of the importance of a banking relationship, an entrepreneur should shop around before making a choice. The criteria for selecting a bank should be based on more than just loan interest rates. Equally important, entrepreneurs should not wait until they have a dire need for funds to try to establish a banking relationship. The choice of a bank and the development of a banking relationship should begin when you don't urgently need the money. When an entrepreneur faces a near-term financial crisis, the venture's financial statements are at their worst and the banker has good cause to wonder about management's financial and planning skills—all to the detriment of the entrepreneur's choices of getting a loan.

Baty and Stancill describe some of the factors that are especially important to an entrepreneur in selecting a bank.[1]

• The bank selected should be big enough to service a venture's forseeable loans but not so large as to be relatively indifferent to your business.

• Banks differ greatly in their desire and capacity to work with small firms. Some banks have special small business loan officers and regard new and early-stage ventures as the seeds of very large future accounts. Other banks see such new venture loans as merely bad risks.

• Does the bank tend to call or reduce its loans to small businesses that have problems? When they have less capital to lend will they cut back on small business loans and favor their older, more solid customers?

• Are they imaginative, creative and helpful when a venture has a problem? To quote Baty, "Do they just look at your balance sheet and faint or do they try to suggest constructive financial alternatives?"

1 G.B. Baty, *Entrepreneurship: Playing to Win* (Reston Publishing Company, 1974); J.M. Stancill, "Getting the Most from Your Banking Relationship," *Harvard Business Review*, March-April 1980.

• Has the bank had lending experience in your industry, and especially with young, developing companies? If they have, your chances of getting a loan are better, and the bank will be more tolerant of problems and better able to help you exploit your opportunities.

• Is there good personal chemistry between you and your prospective lending officer? Remember, the person you talk to and deal with is the bank. Does this person know your industry and competition? Can this officer competently explain your business, technology and uniqueness to other loan officers? Is he/she experienced in administering loans to smaller firms? Can you count on this person consistently? Does he/she have a good track record? Does his or her lending authority meet or exceed your needs? Does he/she have a reputation for being reasonable, creative and willing to take a sound risk?

How does an entrepreneur go about evaluating a bank? First, by consulting accountants, attorneys and other entrepreneurs who have had dealings with the bank. The advice of entrepreneurs who have dealt with a bank through both good and bad times can be especially useful.

Second, by meeting with loan officers at several banks and systematically exploring their attitudes and approaches to their business borrowers. Who meets with you, for how long, and with how many interruptions can be useful measures of a bank's interest in your account.

Finally, ask for small business references from their list of borrowers and talk to the entrepreneurs of those firms. Throughout all of these contacts and discussions, check out particular loan officers as well as the bank itself: he or she is a major determinant of how the bank will deal with you and your venture.

Approaching and Meeting the Banker

Obtaining a loan is a sales job. Many borrowers tends to forget this. An entrepreneur with an early-stage venture must sell himself as well as the viability and potential of his or her business to the banker. This is much the same situation that the early-stage entrepreneur faces with a venture capitalist.

The initial contact with a lender will likely be by telephone. The entrepreneur should be prepared to describe quickly the nature, age and prospects of the venture, the amount of equity financing and who provided it, the prior financial performance of the business, the entrepreneur's experience and background and the sort of bank financing desired. A referral from a venture capital firm or a businessman who knows the banker can be very helpful.

If the loan officer agrees to a meeting, he may well ask that a summary loan proposal, business plan and financial statements be sent ahead of time. A well-prepared business plan and a reasonable amount of equity financing should pique a banker's interest—even for a start-up or very young venture.

The first meeting with a loan officer will likely be at the venture's place of business. The banker will be interested in meeting the management team, seeing how they relate to the entrepreneur, getting a sense of the financial controls and reporting used, and how well things seem to be run. The banker may also want to meet one or more of the venture's equity investors. But most of all, the banker is using this meeting to evaluate the integrity and business acumen of the who will ultimately be responsible for the repayment of the loan.

Throughout meetings with potential bankers, the entrepreneur must convey an air of self-confidence and an optimistic but realistic view of the venture's prospects. If the banker is favorably impressed by what he has seen and read, he will ask for further documents and references and begin to discuss the amount and timing of funds that the bank might lend to the business.

What the Banker Wants to Know

What are you going to do with the money? Does the use of the loan make business sense? Should some or all of the money required be equity capital rather than debt? For new and young businesses, lenders don't like to see total debt to equity ratios greater than one. The answer to this question will also determine the type of loan, e.g., line of credit or term.

How much do you need? You must be prepared to justify the amount requested and describe how the debt fits into an overall plan for financing and developing the business. Further, the amount of the loan should have enough "cushion" to allow for unexpected developments.

Sample of a Summary Loan Proposal

Date of request:	May 30, 1989	
Borrower:	Curtis-Palmer & Company, Inc.	
Amount:	$4,200,000	
Use of Proceeds:	A/R, up to	$1,600,000
	Inventory, up to	824,000
	WIP, up to	525,000
	Marketing, up to	255,000
	Ski show specials	105,000
	Contigencies	50,000
	Officer loans due	841,000
		$4,200,000

Type of loan: Seasonal revolving line of credit
Closing date: June 15, 1989
Term: One year
Rate: Prime + 1%, no compensating balances, no points or origination fees.
Take down: $500,000 at closing
        $1,500,000 on Aug 1, 1989
        $1,500,000 on Oct 1, 1989
        $700,000 on Nov 1, 1989
Collateral: 70% of A/R
                    50% of inventory
Guarantees: None
Repayment schedule: $4,200,000 or balance on anniversary of note
Source of funds   a. Excess cash from operations (see cash
   for repayment: flow)
                    b. Renewal and increase of line if growth is
                        profitable.
                    c. Conversion to three-year note.
Contingency source: a. Sale and leaseback of equipment
                    b. Officer's loans.

When and how will you pay it back? This is an important question. Short term loans for seasonal inventory build-ups or for financing receivables are easier to obtain than long term loans, especially for early-stage businesses. How the loan will be repaid is the "bottom line" question. Presumably you are borrowing money to finance an activity that will throw off enough cash to repay the loan. What is your contingency plan if things go wrong? Can you describe such risks and indicate how you will deal with them? Is there a secondary source of repayment, a guarantor of means?

When do you need the money? If you need the money tomorrow, forget it. You are a poor planner and manager. If, on the other hand, you need the money next month or the month after, you have demonstrated an ability to plan ahead. And you have given the banker time to investigate and process a loan application. Typically, a lending decision can be made in one to three weeks.

One of the best ways for an entrepreneur to answer these questions is by providing the banker with a well-prepared business plan. This plan should contain projections of cash flow, profit and loss, and balance sheets that will demonstrate the need for a loan and how it can be repaid.

A well-prepared business plan is vital for the start-up seeking loans. Particular attention will be given by the lender to such financial ratios as current assets to current liabilities, gross margins, net worth to debt, accounts receivable and payable periods, inventory turns, and net profit to sales. The ratios for the borrower's venture will be compared to averages for competitive firms to see how the potential borrower measures up to them.

For an existing business, the lender will want much of the information that is in a business plan—if not a plan itself. The lender will also want to review financial statements from prior years prepared or audited by a CPA, a list of aged receivables and payables, the turnover of inventory, and lists of key customers and creditors. The lender will also want to know that all tax payments are current. Finally, he will need to know details of fixed assets, and any liens on receivables, inventory or fixed assets.

The entrepreneur-borrower should regard his contacts with the bank as a sales mission and provide data that are required promptly and in a form that can be readily understood. The better the material entrepreneurs can supply to demonstrate their business credibility, the easier and faster it will be to obtain a positive lending decision.

The Lending Decision

Conventional banking wisdom is that lending decisions are based on the "Five Cs of Credit": character, capacity, conditions, capital and collateral. These decision criteria are the same regardless of the size and nature of the business. It is important for entrepreneurs to understand what these five Cs mean to the lender.

Character. Above all else, the banker will only loan money to people he trusts and who impress him as persons of integrity. More specifically, character means two things to a lender. First, that borrowers have the ability and will do everything they can to conserve business assets and repay the loan; money will not be squandered. Second, that when the borrower promises to repay a loan, the borrower means it. And, if this cannot be done, the borrower will have made every possible effort to do so.

Capacity. Does the borrower have the capacity to repay the loan? Does the management have the capacity to use the loan to create the business growth they project?

Conditions. According to many old credit hands, conditions are what change for the worse after the money is loaned. What are the sorts of conditions that an astute lender will consider?

Primarily, whether general business conditions and those within the specific industry of the borrower are such to give the lender pause for concern or optimism. Included in these considerations are the nature of the borrower's product and its competitive position in the marketplace. The lender may well know why a loan to fund the expansion of a business is not a wise move at the time of the loan request.

Capital. Bankers will want to see an adequate amount of equity capital invested in the business from insiders and or outsiders. First, a cash investment by the entrepreneurs and founders is evidence of their faith in the future of the business. Second, there must be sufficient equity capital so that bankers can safely retain their positions as lenders. Without sufficient equity capital (e.g., debt to equity ratio of no more than two), the banker can essentially become a very unwilling shareholder, a position he does not want to be in.

Collateral. The lender must decide whether or not the loan should be collateralized and if so with what. Also, if the lender forecloses on a fixed asset collateral, will its sale at auction cover the loan? To whom can it be sold and for how much? The longer the loan term compared to net worth, the more important the issue of collateral value. Established businesses with high credit ratings do most of their short term borrowings on an unsecured basis. Entrepreneurs with new or early-stage businesses will generally be required to back their loans with all of the assets of their business, key-man life insurance payable to the bank, and personal guarantees.

The Lender's Due Diligence Lending Criteria
- Qualities and qualifications of the management team.
- A business plan which describes:
  –evidence of a market.
  –cash flow, profitability and working capital.
  –specific use of proceeds.
  –accounting systems and controls.
- Availability of timely financial statements.
- A certified audit.
- Adequate debt capacity, in debt coverage (of interest and principal payments) and collateral.
- Demonstrated knowledge of key industry ratios (e.g., Robert Morris Associates data).

12

Borrowing Capital:
After the Loan Decision

Loan Restrictions

A loan agreement defines the terms and conditions under which a lender provides capital. With it, lenders do two things: protect their position as creditor, and try to assure repayment of the loan as agreed.

Within the loan agreement (as in investment agreements) there are negative and positive covenants. Negative covenants are things which the borrower must not do without prior approval of the lender. Examples are no further additions to the borrower's total debt, no pledge to others of assets of the borrower, and no payment of dividends.

Positive covenants define what the borrower must do. Some examples are maintenance of some minimum net worth or working capital, prompt payment of all federal and state taxes, adequate insurance on key people and property, repayment of the loan and interest according to the terms of the agreement, and provision to the lender of periodic financial statements and reports.

Some of these restrictions can hinder a company's growth—for example, a flat restriction on further borrowing. Such a borrowing limit is often based on the borrower's assets at the time of the loan. Rather than an initially fixed limit, the loan agreement should recognize that as a business grows and increases its total assets and net worth, it will need and be able to carry the additional debt required to sustain its growth. Similarly, covenants that require certain minimums on working capital or current ratios may be very difficult for highly seasonable business to maintain at all times of the year. Only an analysis of past financial monthly statements can indicate whether such a covenant can be met.

Covenants to Look Out For

Before borrowing money, an entrepreneur should decide what sorts of restrictions or covenants he or she is prepared to accept. Attorneys and accountants of the company should be consulted before any loan papers are signed. Some restrictions are negotiable, and entrepreneurs should negotiate to get terms that their ventures can live with next year as well as today. Once loan terms are agreed upon and the loan is made, the entrepreneur and his venture will be bound by them.

If the bank says, "Yes, but ..."

- wants to put constraints on your permissible financial ratios.
- won't allow any new borrowing.
- wants a veto on any new management.
- won't allow new products or new directions.
- you can't acquire or sell any assets.
- won't allow any new investment or new equipment.

Personal Guarantees and the Loan

When to Expect Them

- If you are under-collateralized.
- If you have had a poor or erratic performance.
- If you have management problems.
- If your relationship with your banker is strained.
- If you have a new loan officer.
- If there is turbulence in the credit markets.
- If there has been a wave of bad loans made by the lending institution, and a crackdown is in force.

How to Avoid Them

- Good to spectacular performance.
- Conservative financial management.
- Adequate collateral.
- Careful management of the balance sheet.

How to Eliminate Them (if You Already Have Them)

- See above.
- Develop a financial plan with performance targets and a time table.
- Negotiate elimination *up front* when you have some bargaining chips.
- Stay active in the search for back-up sources of funds.

After the Loan: Building a Relationship

After obtaining a loan, entrepreneurs should cultivate a close working relationship with their bankers. Too many businessmen don't see their lending officers until they need a loan. The astute entrepreneur will take a much more active role in keeping a banker informed about the business, thereby improving the chances of obtaining larger loans for expansion, and cooperation from the bank in troubled times.

Some of the things that should be done to build such a relationship are fairly simple (Baty, *op. cit.*) In addition to monthly and annual financial statements, bankers should be sent product news releases and any trade articles about the business or its products. The entrepreneur should invite the banker to the venture's facility and review with him product development plans, the prospects for the business, and any forseeable new loan needs. Above all, the entrepreneur should get the banker interested in the venture and establish a personal relationship with him. If this is done, when a new loan is requested, the lending officer will feel better about recommending its approval.

What about bad news? Never surprise a banker with bad news; make sure he or she sees it coming as soon as you do. Unpleasant surprises are a sign that an entrepreneur is not being candid with his or her banker or that management does not have the business under proper control. Either conclusion by a banker is damaging to the relationship.

If a future loan payment cannot be met, entrepreneurs should not panic and avoid their bankers. On the contrary, they should visit their bankers, explain why a loan payment cannot be made and when it will be made. If this is done before the payment due date and the entrepreneur-banker relationship is good, the banker will go along. After all, what else can he or she do? If an entrepreneur has convinced a banker of the viability and future growth of a business, the banker really does not want to call a loan that could bankrupt it. The real key to communicating with a banker is candidly to inform but not scare. In other words, entrepreneurs must indicate that they are aware of adverse events and have a way of dealing with them.

To further build credibility with bankers, entrepreneurs should borrow before they need to and then repay the loan. This will establish a track record of borrowing and reliable repayment. Entrepreneurs should also make every effort to meet the financial targets they set for themselves and have discused with their banker. If this cannot be done, there will be an erosion of the credibility of the entrepreneur, even if the business is growing.

Bankers have a right to expect an entrepreneur to continue to use them as the business grows and prospers, and not go shopping for a better interest rate. In return, entrepreneurs have the right to expect that their bank will continue to provide them with needed loans, particularly during difficult times when a vacillating loan policy could be dangerous for businesses survival.

The TLC of a Banker or Other Lender

1. Your banker is your partner, not a difficult minority shareholder.
2. Be honest and straightforward in sharing information.
3. Invite the banker to see your business in operation.
4. Always avoid overdrafts, late payments and late financial statements.
5. Answer questions frankly and honestly. *Tell the truth.* Lying is illegal, and undoubtedly violates loan covenants.

What to Do When the Bank Says "No"

What do you do if the bank turns you down for a loan? Regroup, and review the following questions.

1. Does the company really need to borrow now? Can cash be generated elsewhere? Tighten the belt. Are there expenditures that are not really necessary? Sharpen the financial pencil: be lean and mean.

2. What does the balance sheet say? Are you growing too fast? Compare yourself to published industry ratios, to see if you are on target.

3. Does the bank have a clear and comprehensive understanding of your needs? Did you *really* get to know your loan officer? Did you do enough homework on the bank's criteria, their likes and dislikes? Was your loan officer too busy to give your borrowing package proper consideration? A loan officer may have 50 to as many as 200 accounts. Is your relationship with the bank on a proper track?

4. Was your written loan proposal realistic? Was it a normal request, or something that differed from the types of proposals the bank usually sees? Did you make a verbal request for a loan, without presenting any written back-up?

5. Do you need a new loan officer, or a new bank?If your answers to the above questions put you in the clear, and your written proposal was realistic, call the head of the commercial loan department and arrange a meeting. Sit down and discuss the history of your loan effort, the facts, and the bank's reasons for turning you down.

13

Tax-Wise Financing

In recent years several forms of tax-advantaged investment have emerged for financing product development and the start-up of new enterprises. The vehicle used for such investments is the limited partnership. In a general or "ordinary" partnership, all partners have unlimited liability for the actions of the partnership. In a limited partnership there are two classes of partners: general partners and limited partners. Only the general partners have unlimited liability. The liability of the investors is limited to their capital investment.

To qualify for limited liability, the limited partners must not participate in the management of the partnership: the general partners manage its activities. As in a general partnership, there is no tax at the partnership level for gains or losses realized by the limited partnership. Thus, the limited partnership offers the best of both worlds to its investors: limited liability and a single level of taxation.

There is yet another advantage to the limited partnership. Gains and losses may be allocated differently to the limited and general partners. For example, the limited partners may be allocated 90% of the losses and 40% of the profits and capital gains of the partnership. This permits high tax-bracket investors to expense for tax purposes most of the losses generally associated with product development and/or starting a new company, and reduces their capital risk.

(A Subchapter S corporation also provides single-level taxation and limited liability. However, the number of investors in a Subchapter S corporation is limited to 25, including all shareholders or partners of an investing entry, and it does not allow for a different allocation of gains and losses—that is, shareholders are allocated both gains and losses in direct proportion to their shareholdings. Notwithstanding this, a Subchapter S can provide some tax advantage to start-up investors.)

The astute entrepreneur may well ask: why not make the general partner a corporation and thereby limit the liability of all partners in a limited partnership? Unfortunately, the IRS has also thought of this. To ensure that a limited partnership with a *sole corporate general partner* is not a "sham" for tax purposes, the IRS has adapted two "safe harbor rules" that such a limited partnership should meet if it is to be taxed as a partnership:

1. *Ownership requirements*. The limited partners may not own more than 20% of the corporate general partner. This ownership may be in shares, or may be interpreted as a percentage of contributed capital only if the limited partners have made a cash or in-kind investment. In other words, the corporate general partner must have real assets which are at least four times any investment in it by the limited partners.

2. *Capital requirements*. If the capital invested in the partnership is more than $2.5 million, the corporate general partner must have a net worth of at least 10% of the partnership's capital at all times. For capital investments less than $2.5 million, the corporate general partner must have a net worth of 15% of the partnership's capital, but no more than $250,000.

The above rules are only guidelines or opinions issued by the IRS and do not appear in any formal tax regulations. Nevertheless, most limited partnerships with a sole corporate general partner will attempt to meet these conditions. The tax considerations are sufficiently complex that an entrepreneur should not set up a limited partnership without expert legal advice. It is essential that the limited partnership be treated for tax purposes as a partnership and not a corporation by the IRS if the limited partners are to receive tax benefits.

The two forms of tax-sheltered investment vehicles that are most popular and most used are the "equity partnership" and the "R&D (research and development) partnership."

Equity Partnerships

The equity partnership is used to start up and operate a business. The basic notion is to flow losses to the limited partners during the start-up and early development phases of a business. Once the venture product is developed and the business seems to be moving toward profitability, the partnership may assume corporate form, with the limited partners becoming shareholders of the corporation which succeeds the partnership.

In most equity partnerships, a corporation serves as the general partner with the entrepreneurs as shareholders. The investors in equity partnerships are primarily interested in long-term capital gains, and view the tax shelter features of the vehicle as a way of reducing their capital risk. Several venture capital firms specialize in investing as a limited partner in equity partnerships. Among them are Venture Founders Corporation of Waltham, Massachusetts, and Crosspoint Ventures of Palo Alto, California.

The legal documents associated with an equity partnership can be complex. In spite of this, an equity partnership can be advantageous to the entrepreneur. First, because investors are receiving tax write-offs for part or all of their investment and reducing their capital risk, the entrepreneur can usually get start-up financing for less equity than would be given to investors in a corporate vehicle.

Second, the potential tax savings to investors can serve to stimulate seed and start-up investments by wealthy individual investors. The main disadvantages to the equity partnership are its complexity and the loss of future tax-loss carryforwards by a successor corporation. The risk of having such tax losses disallowed lies with the limited partner investors.

Research and Development Partnerships

Research and development partnerships are used by both start-up and established businesses to fund the development of a product. An existing sponsor corporation identifies a product research or development program that it wants to fund without showing the expenditures on its income statement. A limited partnership is organized to fund the sponsoring corporation to conduct the work. The limited partnership makes payments to the corporation for the work it conducts and the investors receive the benefit of tax deductions for research and development expenses.

If the research and development is successful, ownership of the products resides with the limited partnership. Generally, the limited partnership grants the sponsor corporation an option to acquire the technology or product in return for pre-negotiated royalties on subsequent sales. Royalties paid to the limited partners can be treated as capital gains, if the option is a real one and not exercisable until at least six months after completion of the research and development. The limited partnership must be seen to bear the risk of the work.

In a typical research and development partnership, the limited partners will have tax write-offs for 70% to 90% of the partners' capital and royalties may run 7% to 10%.

Research and development partnerships have acquired a certain notoriety: Storage Technology used one to fund the development of a computer which it later abandoned, and John DeLorean used one for developing his automobile. Smaller companies with smaller financing requirements have also used them. Most recently, Telesis raised a $4.5 million partnership to fund the development of new projects.

A research and development partnership has several disadvantages for the new venture. The future payment of royalties can significantly reduce a company's ability to produce cash and profits. Further, an overhanging future royalty payment can be a negative factor in a future equity-financing decision by a venture capital firm, because it reduces profitability. As with an equity partnership, an entrepreneur should obtain expert and specialized legal and accounting advice before setting up a research and development partnership.

14

Federal and State Financing

In the 1970s there were a number of loan-guarantee, direct loan and grant programs from at least five federal agencies. Only two have survived into the 1980s: the direct loan and loan guarantee programs of the SBA (Small Business Administration), and the SBIR (Small Business Innovation Research program).

Small Business Administration

The SBA is often the lender of last resort for entrepreneurs who have been unable to obtain bank loans or other financing. SBA small business loans are used to finance plant construction or expansion, to purchase equipment and to provide working capital.

For SBA purposes, a small business is defined as one that is not dominant in its industry; is independently owned and operated; has a net worth less than $6 million; and has after-tax profits for its last two years that average less than $2 million. About 95% of all businesses in the United States are small by SBA standards.

The SBA provides annually about $2.5 billion in loans and loan guarantees to about 25,000 businesses, of which about 6,000 to 7,000 are new businesses. The SBA offers two types of loans: guaranteed and direct.

Guaranteed loans are made by a bank, and the SBA guarantees a large portion of each loan: 70% to 90% of loans over $100,000, and 90% of loans under $100,000. Almost 80% of all SBA financial assistance is in the form of loan guarantees, and loans up to $500,000 can be guaranteed by the SBA. To be eligible for a guaranteed loan, the borrower must have been denied loans by two banks.

Direct loans are made by the SBA to the borrower. These loans are not available unless the borrower has been rejected by two banks for a loan with an SBA guarantee. These loans are limited to $150,000, and are hard to obtain because federal funding for them is limited. Direct loans may be the only financing some businesses can get, and certainly carry substantial risk for the SBA.

SBA business loans can have terms that range from a short period of time to ten years. In some cases, the term can be extended beyond ten years. The banks' interest rate on guaranteed loans is within reasonable limits set by the SBA and is, typically, one to two percent over prime. Interest rates on direct loans are set by the government, and are prime or less.

Applying for SBA Small Business Loans

The following are the step-by-step procedures for applying for SBA loans or loan guarantees by an established business or a new business. Applications for SBA loans are made by using SBA Form 4 (direct loan application) or Form 4-I (guaranteed bank loan), along with a statement of personal history.

For new businesses

1. Describe in detail the type of business to be established.
2. Describe the experience and capabilities of management.
3. Prepare an estimate of how much you or others can invest in the business and how much you must borrow.
4. Prepare a current financial statement (balance sheet) listing all personal assets and liabilities. Prepare a detailed projection of earnings for the first year of operation.
5. List the collateral to be offered as security for the loan, with your estimate of the present market value of each item.

For established businesses

1. Prepare a current financial statement (balance sheet) listing all assets and all liabilities of the business. Do not include personal items.
2. Have an earnings (profit and loss) statement for the previous full year and for the current period to the date of the balance sheet.
3. Prepare a current personal financial statement of the owner, or of each partner or stockholder owning 20% or more of the corporate stock in the business.

4. List the collateral to be offered as security for the loan, with your estimate of the present market value of each item.
5. State the amount of the loan required and explain the exact purpose for which it will be used.

For both

Take this material with you and see your banker. Ask for a direct bank loan and, if declined, ask the bank to make the loan under the SBA Loan Guaranty Plan or to participate with the SBA in a loan. If the bank is interested in an SBA guaranty or participation loan, ask the banker to contact the SBA for discussion of your application. In most cases of guaranty or participation loans, the SBA will deal directly with the bank.

If a guaranty or participation loan is not available, write or visit the nearest SBA office to apply for a direct loan. SBA has 79 field offices and, in addition, sends loan officers to visit many smaller cities on a regularly scheduled basis or as need arises. To speed matters, make your financial information available when you first write or visit SBA.

The advantage of an SBA loan is that it may be "the only game in town." What are some of the disadvantages? Personal guarantees from anyone owning more than 20% of the business. A first lien on "all" assets of the company. Restrictions on the amounts that can be spent for assets without SBA and/or bank approval. And finally, the amount of time that it can take to get SBA financing—two to four months in metropolitan areas.

Small Business Innovation Research Program

Under the Small Business Innovation Development Act, all federal government agencies with research and development budgets in excess of $100 million must establish SBIR programs. The funding of each SBIR program is a fixed percentage of each agency's research and development budget. There are now twelve agencies participating in the program.

The SBIR program provides small, technology-based businesses with an opportunity to obtain grants to finance innovative projects that meet the federal government's research and development needs and, at the same time, have commercial potential.

The SBIR program consists of three phases. Phase 1 is to evaluate the scientific/technical merit and feasibility of an idea. Financing for this phase is up to $50,000.

Phase 2 continues the development started in Phase 1. Awards are based on the results of the earlier phase, and generally also require an expression of interest in future financing from a private source. If the Phase 2 work is successful, awards of up to $500,000 may be made in this phase. Only Phase 1 awardees are eligible for Phase 2 awards.

Phase 3 involves the commercialization of the technology and/or products developed in Phase 2 and requires the use of non-government funding. Ideally, it is hoped that a venture capital firm will provide financing.

Only small for-profit businesses with 500 or fewer employees are eligible to receive SBIR awards.

The SBIR program was initiated by the National Science Foundation (NSF) in the late 1970s. In 1987, $500 million was awarded. Thus, the SBIR program should become an interesting source of seed funds for technology-oriented businesses.

To apply for an SBIR, entrepreneurs should contact the agency representative listed below for a delineation of the research and technology topics of potential interest to each of them. A proposal of no more than 25 pages should be prepared which describes the approach to be used and the qualifications of the people who will do it. A Phase 2 proposal should also indicate the commercial potential and who the Phase 3 financing source might be. Proposals are competitively evaluated to determine the best innovative solutions to an agency's technical topic.

SBIR Representatives at Participating Agencies

Dr. Carl Schwenk
National Aeronautics and Space
Administration
SBIR Office—Code RB
600 Independence Avenue S.W.
Washington DC 20546
(202) 453-2848

Dr. W. K. Murphey
Office of Grants
and Program Systems
Department of Agriculture
West Auditors
Building, Rm. 112
15th&Independence Ave S.W.
Washington DC 20251
(202) 475-5022

Roland Tibbetts
Ritchie Coryell
SBIR Program Managers
National Science Foundation
1800 G Street N.W.
Washington DC 20550
(202) 357-7527

James P. Maruca
Director, Office of Small
and Disadvantaged Business
Utilization
Department of Commerce, Room
6411
14th&Constitution Ave. N.W.
Washington DC 20230
(202) 377-1472

Wayne Batson
Office of Nuclear
Regulatory Research
Nuclear Regulatory Commission
Washington DC 20460
(301) 427-4250

Horace Crouch
Director, Small Business
and Economic Utilization
Office of Secretary of Defense
Room 2A340—The Pentagon
Washington DC 20301
(202) 697-9383

Dr. Edward Esty
SBIR Program Coordinator
Office of Educational
Research and Improvement
Department of Education,
Mail Stop 402
Washington DC 20208
(202) 254-8247

Dr. Thomas Henrie
Chief Scientist
U. S. Department
of the Interior
401 E Street N.W.
Washington DC 20241
(202) 634-1305

Ms. Gerry Washington
c/o SBIR Program Manager
U. S. Department of Energy
Washington DC 20545
(301) 353-5867

George Kovatch
SBIR Program Manager
Transportation Systems Center
Department of Transportation
Kendall Square
Cambridge MA 02142
(617) 494-2051

Walter H. Preston
Office of Research
and Development
Environmental
Protection Agency
401 M Street S.W.
Washington DC 20460
(202) 382-5744

Mr. Richard Clinkscales
Director, Office of Small
and Disadvantaged
Business Utilization
Department of Health
and Human Services
200 Independence Ave. S.W.
Room 513D
Washington DC 20201
(202) 245-7300

State Sources

Almost every state has a program for providing financial assistance to help companies start up or expand within the state. Some states are more active than others. Although state programs are principally intended for existing businesses, increasing interest is being directed toward start-ups. The states want such programs to promote economic development and create jobs within the state.

There are basically three types of *direct* financial-aid programs. The first are administered by state agencies created to provide direct loans, loan guarantees and sometimes equity capital to businesses. A second form of state aid is provided through Business Development Corporations (BDCs). At any one time about 25 to 30 states have active BDCs.

A BDC is a privately owned corporation authorized by the state to promote and assist in the growth and development of businesses in the state. Its capital comes from the sale of stock and/or loans made to the BDC by financial institutions and private individuals. BDCs can also obtain funds from the SBA which may only be used to help small businesses.

BDCs generally make loans and sometimes provide equity capital to businesses that are too marginal to obtain funds from a bank. Interest rates on loans can range from below prime to four percent or so over prime. BDC and/or state agency loans are generally for equipment purchases, facility improvements, new buildings and sometimes working capital. A BDC normally requires the same sort of information from an applicant that a commercial bank requires.

In the smaller states, BDCs can be a very active financing source. In Wyoming, for example, the BDC is the most active financial institution in the state and has provided all of the financing for some start-ups.

The third state financing program is the Industrial Revenue Bond (IRB). These bonds are a common form of state financial assistance. IRBs are issued by a state or municipality and use the funds raised to construct or expand plant facilities which are leased to a business. After the bonds are paid back from the lease payments, the user can renew the lease for long periods at favorable rates.

It is important to note that the credit supporting these bonds are the lease payments of the renter. Hence, IRBs will generally only be issued to build facilities for a firm with an excellent credit rating.

Obtaining financing from any of the above state sources requires a great deal of patience. Things don't happen quickly in a state bureaucracy. The financial assistance programs available in each state and who to contact about them change over time. The most recent compilation of whom to contact can be found in *Sources of Federal and State Financing* (1988, Venture Economics, Needham MA).

15

Negotiating the Deal

When the venture capital investor has decided to go ahead with an investment, negotiations will begin with the entrepreneur on the terms of that investment. These negotiations normally are handled by a senior member of the venture capital firm and the president of the venture. In the case of an investment by a syndicate of venture capital firms, one firm will serve as the "lead investor" and conduct negotiations for the investor group.

What is Negotiable?

The answer to this question is, far more than you may have thought. There are a wide range of issues that come up and are negotiable. A normal ploy for attorneys representing the investors is to insist that "this is our standard deal; we always have these clauses or terms in our investment agreements." Yet, if you have assessed your bargaining position as healthy—i.e., you have other, enthusiastic sources—you can negotiate, and craft the agreement to meet your needs rather than accept the so-called "boilerplate" as is.[1]

The negotiables include:

• The basic valuation of the company: how much equity is relinquished for the money the investor puts in?

• Who will pay the legal and accounting fees necessary to complete the deal?

• What type of stock will be issued? Investors may want to purchase a convertible preferred stock, while the entrepreneur prefers to issue common stock or debt plus stock.

• Will management remain as is? Investors may want a management change if they believe the venture team to be lacking in some skill, or if

1 See, for example, H. M. Hoffman and J. Blakey, "You Can Negotiate with Venture Capitalists," *Harvard Business Review*, March-April 1987.

they think that someone else in the team should be president of the company instead of its current leader. You may or may not go along with this.

• How many directors' seats will be allocated to investors? This is often perceived by the entrepreneur as a control issue, but is in fact usually not so. Management controls a business. Venture investors will not try to intervene unless a business seriously fails to perform as planned. In such a case, the investors may seek management changes via the board of directors.

• Will investors have registration rights for their stock in the case of a registered public offering? Underwriters will generally limit the investor's stock coming onto the market with the first public offering.

• Will investors have first refusal on subsequent stock offerings? This can be troublesome if earlier stockholders had no such rights.

• Will there be stock-vesting agreements? In this case, the entrepreneurs do not own all their stock initially but acquire ownership over a period extending from three to five years.

• Will there be employment contracts, non-compete and proprietary rights agreements between you and the venture you have proposed? Non-compete agreements are generally insisted on by venture capitalists.

• Are there any other terms or clauses you believe are potentially burdensome?

It is very important that you and your management work out your positions on these and other issues beforehand. On price per share paid by the investor, entrepreneurs should decide what they would like to get and what they will accept.

During the negotiation, the investors will be evaluating your negotiating skills, intelligence and maturity. This gives you an opportunity to do precisely same with them. If they are arrogant, overly demanding, unwilling to give an inch or compromise, and seem bent on getting every last drop out of the deal, while locking you into as many tough clauses as possible, then you "ain't seen nothing yet!" Wait until you hit some rough business weather.

Terms Sheet

Once investors and entrepreneur reach agreement, a terms sheet is usually drafted that describes the main features of the investment in plain language. This document defines and summarizes the basic "handshake" agreeement resulting from the negotiations. It spells out the valuation and the allocation among parties. It summarizes tehkey financial and legal terms agreed upon. It may also impose certain legal obligations on both parties if the deal does not close.

Most important, it serves as an early detector of "deal-killers" beyond the basic valuation, such as buy-back and forfeiture restrictions, composition of the Board of Directors, and the employment, confidentiality, stock-vesting and proprietary rights agreements.

The terms sheet is then given to an attorney, who prepares an investment agreement. The deal is not closed until the formal investment agreement is signed by both parties.

A successful negotiation is one in which both the entrepreneur and the investor believe they have made a "fair deal." More important than a few percentage points of ownership one way or the other is a constructive working relationship between the entrepreneur and the investor.

Valuation and Investor Equity

The key issue in negotiating a deal is the valuation of investor equity. Generally, the later the stage of development of a business, the smaller the percentage of ownership the venture capitalist expects to receive for a given dollar investment.

The usual negotiation ranges are 40–70% or more for the venture capital investor who puts in all the required funds when a venture is in start-up, and 10–40% for ventures beyond start-up, the percentage depending on the amount invested and the maturity and track record of the venture.

If the entrepreneurial team is investing capital at the same time as the venture capitalist, that money should buy stock on the same terms as that of the investor. This purchased stock is added to that received by the entrepreneurs for their nonfinancial contributions.

Most venture capital investors, even those investing at very early stages, recognize the incentive value of the entrepreneurial team's equity position. Thus, most venture capitalists will leave entrepreneurs and their team with an attractive share of the venture or options or warrants to buy that share. What "attractive" means is negotiable; but few venture capital investors would dilute an entrepreneurial team below 20–25% of their venture at the start-up stage for fear of diluting their commitment to the venture.

In a leveraged buyout, in contrast, the entire management team might end up with 15–25% of the ownership. The remainder will be required by the sources of equity and debt capital, since very large amounts are provided compared to the amounts management is normally able to contribute.

Some of the factors that may persuade a venture capitalist to take less than typical ownership in a start-up or first-stage venture are:

- Previous profit responsibility and above-average profit or harvest performance by the lead entrepreneur.
- The presence of a complete management team, which means less risk for the investor.
- An entrepreneurial team with in-depth and up-to-date knowledge of their target market and substantial previous experience in selling to, and getting orders from, the venture's prospective customers.
- A demonstrably strong position for the venture's product or service in terms of patent know-how, exclusive market, lead time.
- The likelihood that substantial additional equity funding will be needed within the next 18 to 24 months, which will dilute the entrepreneurial team's percentage ownership below the level at which they feel that they have a real stake in the business.

In one deal in the cellular communcations industry in which I am involved, the management team is considered to be industry "superstars." The backers therefore were willing to split the equity 50–50, even though management invested no money.

At any stage of a company's development the percentage of equity purchased by the investor is a result of negotiation. The starting point may be an analysis of the current and projected value of the venture and the return on investment objectives of the investor. But, ultimately, this issue of venture valuation is a subjective one that depends as much as anything else on the value being given to ventures of similar age, technology and potential by the marketplace of venture capital investors at that time.

Before approaching a venture investor, entrepreneurs would do well to determine what their desired valuation means in terms of pre-financing valuation. For example, if you are trying to raise $2 million for 50% of your company you are saying that its value before any money is invested is $2 million. Can you justify that figure? Many entrepreneurs cannot.

A Valuation Example

How might investors determine a starting point for negotiating the equity they want for their investment? Suppose a company projects after-tax profits in three years at $175,000, and that potential investors believe it. Other companies in the same industry are generally valued by investors at six to eight times after-tax earnings. Based on these assumptions, the "value" of the venture being considered in year three would be:

$175,000 times 6 to 8 = $1,050,000 to $1,400,000

Two more assumptions are (a) the investor is considering a $200,000 investment and (b) the investor wants a 40% annual return on the original investment over three years. The $200,000 invested would thus be worth approximately $550,000 at the end of year three. The ratios of return to value at year three are thus $500,000/$1.4 million to $500,000/$1.05 million, or 39% to 52%.

The "present value" formula underlies this example, where PV = present value, FV = future value, i = investment rate of return, and n = number of years the investment is held, or

$$PV = FV / (1 + i)^n$$

Thus

$$\$200,000 = FV/(1.40)3 = FV/2.744$$

$$FV = \$548,800, \text{ rounded to } \$550,000$$

Such valuations are only a starting point because they are based on earnings projections which are reasoned hopes and, usually, unreliable. This is especially true for start-ups that have little or no record of sales or earnings. For this reason, the venture capitalists' valuation of start-ups and early stage deals is highly subjective and largely dependent on the valuation accorded other venture capital deals of the same kind.

In order to obtain a target return, venture capital investors invest so that they get—or can get—equity. Debt, by definition, has a fixed return, which is usually not at the level desired by the venture capital investors.

16

Structuring the Investment

What is meant by "deal structure"? There are several components:
- Who gets what ownership.
- The cost.
- Legal control of the company.
- Terms, instruments and conditions.
- Rights and obligations of founders and investors.

One central question you must address is what ownership (share of my equity) do I give up and what will I get for it? What you get will be direct common-stock ownership; rights, via preferred shares or warrants, to convert common-stock ownership; or some other mechanism that creates a claim on the profit, cash flow stream or sometimes the revenue stream (i.e., a royalty, license fee or portion of sales).

An equally—and some entrepreneurs would say more—important issue is voting control of the company. Various covenants and clauses to an agreement spell out the rights and obligations of each party. These define who will have control of the company, and under what conditions. The specific voting rights, conversion rights, board seats, employment, stock vesting and non-compete agreements, and any debt guarantees are defined in the deal structure.

As a matter of practice, the better outside investors do not want to run or control your company. After all, they bet on you and your management team, and strive to make sure that substantial ownership incentives exist in the deal to motivate and reward the team. Except for very early stage, unusually risky seed and start-up deals (or where huge amounts of capital are needed for an LBO or an MBO), the investors will not even require a majority ownership position.

In today's risk capital market it is safe to say that virtually all deal structures provide the outside investor with a safety valve: if exisiting management cannot achieve the agressive sales and earnings objectives agreed upon, then outside minority owners will have a mechanism in the deal structure to gain the majority of board votes necessary to replace what they believe is inadequate management. This is not to be taken lightly: management replacements have become more commonplace in recent years.

Instruments Used

There are three instruments generally used by venture capitalists for early-stage venture investments: common stock, convertible preferred stock and subordinated debt.

Common stock is often used in venture capital financing. Common-stock holders have the right to vote on such issues as the composition of the board of directors. They also have the right to the earnings and assets of the firm only after all expenses, debt and other obligations have been met.

Thus, in most venture situations, the common-stock investor has little chance to recoup any of the investment if the business moves sideways or fails. On the positive side, the purchase of common stock gives the venture capital investor the most equity for the invested dollar and a large potential for capital gain.

Convertible preferred stock, in a venture capital financing, is convertible into a number of common stock shares at the option of the investor. Generally, the number of common shares received per share of preferred stock is adjusted upwards if stock is subsequently sold at a lower per-share price than that of the preferred. This instrument can include voting control over the majority of common shares if performance expectations are not met.

Preferred-share holders have a preference over common-stock holders (generally management), but not debtors, in the event of liquidation of the company. Sometimes, five to ten years after the investment date, the company may be required to redeem at an appreciated value shares of preferred that have not been converted. Currently, convertible preferred stock is the favored form of investment for start-ups and early-stage deals.

Subordinated debt provides the venture capital investor with the advantages of a debt instrument without restricting a venture's ability to obtain senior debt from banks. It is usually considered equity by such senior lenders as long as it does not dominate the balance sheet.

If things don't go well, subordinated debt gives the venture capitalist greater protection than afforded common or preferred stockholders. One way investors obtain this protection is through an accelerated payment clause in the indenture (debt) agreement that makes the full amount of the loan payable within a specified time of a venture's failure to comply with certain agreed-upon conditions. These conditions might include the venture's agreeing to maintain minimum working capital or agreeing not to merge or sell certain assets.

Because a young venture is not likely to be able to retire the debt, the investor has the power to bankrupt the venture if it doesn't change its operations to meet the terms of the debt agreement. However, we should note that venture capital investors do not want to ruin ventures in which they invest. They resort to this only to protect their investment.

A venture capital investor will generally issue subordinated debt with a stock convertible feature or warrants to purchase stock. Either of these arrangements provides the venture capital investor with a future option to obtain common stock and realize the greater-than-normal return that accrues to equity owners in a successful company. At the same time, the venture capitalist can receive interest payments on the debt and has a higher call than common or preferred stock on the assets of a company in the event of liquidation.

The difference between convertible subordinated debt and subordinated debt with warrants should be noted. If the warrants are nondetachable, they are equivalent to a conversion feature and the stock must be purchased before the debt is repaid. However, if the warrants are detachable, then the stock purchase can be made before or after the debt is repaid, providing the exercise time of the warrants has not run out.

Investment Agreements: An Overview

No investment agreement will make a good deal out of a bad one; but it could do the opposite if not properly drawn. Investment agreements are complex, and entrepreneurs should make sure that the attorneys they consult are experienced in preparing them. Experienced means having prepared, negotiated and lived with at least a dozen or more deals over several years, including both liquidations and harvests. Preferably, at least some of these deals should be in the general technology and market niche you are in. Without such experience, the attorney's cost to a venture could be far more than just a legal fee.

The investment agreement is the document that defines the terms and conditions upon which an investor or investors will make a substantial investment in a venture. If prepared properly, the investment agreement should accomplish the following objectives:

- Define the amount, type, terms and timing of the investment (stock, convertible debentures, notes, warrants, etc.)
- Provide terms that will motivate and retain the entrepreneurial team if they perform as planned.
- Provide "downside protection" to investors by giving them control of the venture if it is in danger of failing.
- Provide and protect opportunities for the investor to realize capital gains and liquidity.

In order to meet these objectives, the investment agreement must anticipate and consider a number of future, contingent events. The resulting document can be lengthy and contain issues that may not have been explicitly discussed during negotiations. The entrepreneur and an attorney who is very experienced in such deals should review it carefully and reopen discussions with the investor on any aspects that are unacceptable.

There are seven basic categories of terms, conditions, and representations in an investment agreement.

Description of the investment defines the basic terms of the investment. This includes the parties to the agreement; the kind, amount, and price of securities to be issued; and the description of the collateral, guarantees, or subordination associated with debt. If the investment involves warrants for stock or debt conversion privileges, the terms (time limits, price, etc.) of these will be completely described.

Preconditions to closing are things the venture must do, or supplementary data and agreements it must submit to the investor before the investment can be closed. Examples are the execution of employment contracts or the venture's securing a line of credit.

Representations and warranties are legally binding statements made by the venture's officers that describe its condition on or before the closing date. For example, the venture will warrant that it is a duly organized corporation in good standing with assets as represented on financial statements.

Although most warranties and representations are made by the venture, there are some that must be made by the investor. For example, if the securities are sold via a private placement, the investor will warrant that the stock is being acquired solely for investment and not with a view to resale or distribution.

Affirmative covenants define what the venture must do to run its business in a manner that is acceptable to the investor. Requirements to have investors on the venture's board of directors are examples of affirmative covenants.

Negative covenants define what the venture must not do or must not do without the prior approval of the investor. Restrictions on loans and management salaries are typical negative covenants.

Conditions of default describe those events that constitute a breach of the investment agreement if not corrected within a specified time. One condition of default is a failure to comply with the affirmative or negative covenants.

Remedies are actions that an investor may take in the event default has occurred. Remedies can include acceleration of debt repayment, forfeiture of escrowed stock or temporary voting rights to control the company's board of directors.

In addition to the investment agreement, the closing of the deal generally involves the execution of a number of ancillary agreements. Such agreements might include non-compete agreements with the entrepreneurial team and employment and stock-vesting agreements with key personnel.

Stock vesting agreements define how much of an entrepreneur's stock is subject to repurchase at cost if the entrepreneur leaves the employ of the venture for any reason. Generally, an entrepreneur's stock in an early-stage venture will not be fully vested (subject to repurchase) until 3 to 5 years after the closing of an investment.

Supplementary agreements may also be used to give investors preemptive rights (to maintain their percentage ownership of the venture), and rights to include their stock in registered public stock offerings of the venture and to demand one or more registrations for their stock.

Potentially Burdensome Conditions

There are several conditions that attorneys representing the investors may attempt to include in the investment agreement. It is a good idea to keep an eye out for them, and to make sure you and your attorney understand their business implications. Which ones are finally included in the deal are a matter of negotiation, as was pointed out in the previous chapter. There may be others that are equally burdensome, given the unique nature of your company and situation, but the following are worth flagging:

• *Participating preferred stock.* Investors are repaid first (purchase price plus accrued dividends) in the case of liquidation. In addition, holders of participating preferred stock share (on a pro rata basis) with the common-stock holders (founders) any remaining assets. Founders end up with much less, therefore, than do the outside investors.

• *Antidilution "ratchet-down" provision.* Lead investor is issued additional common stock if the company completes any subsequent sales of stock at a lower price. If investors hold convertible preferred stock, the conversion price is adjusted to equal the lower sales price.

• *Antidilution "weighted average" or "formula" provision.* Has a less drastic effect than the above, but still can lower the entrepreneur's stake. Conversion price is adjusted based on a weighted average formula (the formula considers the price of each stock issuance).

• *Demand registration rights.* Investors can demand that their shares be registered for public sale (typically within the next three to five years). Realistically, demand rights are hard to invoke, although their presence may influence a company's decision to go public.

• *Piggy-back registration rights.* Grants investors (but not necessarily the entrepreneur) the right to include their shares in any stock registration the company undertakes. As a practical matter, these rights are typically unenforceable, as the underwriters "control" the offering.

• *Mandatory redemption of preferred stock ("put option")*. Company must buy out the investors if the company fails to complete an IPO (or other harvest) within a specified time period. The company needs to consider where the cash will come from.

• *Co-sale provision*. Investors can tender their shares if the founders sell additional stock before an IPO. Causes conflicts with later-round investors; inhibits the ability of the founders to cash out.

• *Forced buyout*. If management doesn't find a buyer or hasn't taken the company public by a certain date, investors can find a buyer.

• *Washout financing*. Strategy of last resort. "Washes out" (dilutes) all previously issued stock (preferred shareholders and/or founders) when existing shareholders won't commit additional funds.

• *Key person insurance*. Is company or preferred shareholders the payee? Investors often require a policy payable directly to them with a face amount equal to their investment.

The Entrepreneur's Decision

If their venture and management team are particularly attractive, entrepreneurs may find that they have more offers of venture capital than they need. How do they decide which to accept? In this situation, they should ask themselves: What value beyond money can a particular venture capitalist bring to the venture? Then they should pick those that can provide assistance other than invested capital.

The right venture capitalist can add value in a number of ways. Principal among these are identifying and helping to recruit key management team members; serving as a sounding board for ideas and plans to solve problems or quicken growth; helping to establish relationships with key customers and/or suppliers; and having "deep pockets" to participate in and syndicate subsequent rounds of financing.

If a choice of venture capitalists is available, an entrepreneur should check out potential investors by talking to the founders of successful and unsuccessful companies that they have backed. Entrepreneurs should also check a venture capitalist's reputation in the financial community.

There will likely not be a unanimity of opinion, but a picture should emerge of which investors are passive and which are helpful, active investors.[1]

Entrepreneurs should seek to strike a deal with venture capitalists who can provide contacts and helpful expertise as well as capital; who can provide additional financing when and if required; and who are patient and interested in the long-term development of the company.

Inevitably entrepreneurs will receive investment offers that place a lower valuation on their venture than they think it merits. How far entrepreneurs should compromise on the valuation of their deal depends partially on the attractiveness of the venture and heavily on the availability of venture capital for early-stage ventures.

In times of bear markets for new issues when venture capital for early-stage ventures tends to dry up, entrepreneurs may have to accept a good deal less money for the equity offered than they would like, if financing is to be obtained at all for their venture. In such a case, they might elect to curtail their operations and wait for a more favorable investment climate. On the other hand, in times of a bull market in new issues and speculative activity, entrepreneurs can obtain investment terms that are much more favorable.

When the final negotiations are underway, the entrepreneur is usually at a considerable disadvantage in bargaining power. As one experienced venture capital attorney, Sandy Taylor, put it, "I've been on both sides of the table, and I'd rather be on the side of the venture capitalist any day of the week. It does not matter what the entrepreneur's attorney argues, I know I hold all the trump cards."

1 See J. A. Timmons, "Venture Capital: More Than Money?" in *Pratt's Guide to Venture Capital Sources*, 13th ed., 1989 (Venture Economics, Wellesley MA).

17

Harvest and Beyond

More than any other single issue, the harvest separates the real entrepreneurs from the rest of the pack. It is one thing to create a job and a good living for yourself, but it is quite another to do so for many others, including investors. Having a harvest mindset, anchored in a goal of growing a business that creates enough value to result in a capital gain, is central to entrepreneurial achievement.

Why is a Harvest Important?

A harvest mindset necessitates a compelling long-term goal to create real added value in whatever business you choose to grow. Such a goal creates a high standard and a serious commitment to excellence. It can also provide a motivating force and a strategic focus that does not sacrifice customers, employees and products and services just to maximize quarterly earnings.

There are other good reasons as well. The demanding workload is probably no greater in a harvest-oriented venture than in one that cannot achieve a harvest, and it may actually be less. Nor is it necessarily any more stressful, and may actually be less.

Imagine the plight of the entrepreneur with three children in college whose business is overleveraged and on the brink of collapse. Contrast that frightful pressure with the position of the founder and major stockholder of one venture who, at the same age, recently sold his venture for $15 million.

Consider the options now available to the two entrepreneurs. The choices open to the harvested entrepreneur—compared to one who has not or cannot reap a substantial profit—seem to rise geometrically. The marketplace has responded; other investors, entrepreneurs, and bankers also respond with new opportunities. Given these factors, is there really a serious choice in the matter?

Finally, there is a very significant societal reason for seeking and building a venture worthy of a harvest. These are the ventures that provide enormous impact and added value in a variety of ways. These are the companies that contribute most disproportinately to technological innovation, to new jobs, to returns for investors, and to economic vibrancy. Within the process of harvest, the seeds of renewal and reinvestment are laid. Such a recyling of entrepreneurial talent and capital is at the very heart of our system of private responsibility for economic renewal and individual initiative.

The Harvest Options

There are six principal avenues by which a company can realize a harvest from the value it has created. These are listed below in the order in which they most commonly seem to occur, thereby creating a determinable value for the founder's stock. You will note that a harvest need not necessarily mean having to sell and leave the company. Each of these paths will be discussed briefly below. (Since there are books written entirely on each of these types of harvest, including their legal, tax and accounting intricacies, it is not possible to do more here than alert you to the key issues.)

The Capital Cow. The "capital cow" is to the entrepreneur what the "cash cow" is to the large corporation. In essence, the high-margin, profitable venture throws off more cash for personal use than most entrepreneurs have the time, uses and inclinations to spend it on. The result is a capital and cash-rich company with enormous capacity for debt and reinvestment.

Take, for instance, one firm, a health-care related venture which was started in the early 1970s, realized early success and actually went public back then. Several years later the founders decided to buy the company back from the public shareholders and to return it to its closely held status.

Today the company is a Subchapter S corporation (fewer than 25 shareholders, limited liability, and no corporate income tax obligation) with sales in excess of $100 million. It has generated extra capital in excess of $3 million or so each year. This "capital cow" has enabled the entrepreneurs to invest in several other high-potential ventures, including the leveraged buyout of a $150 million sales division of a larger firm.

The Employee Stock Ownership Plan. The ESOP has become very popular among closely held companies as a way to put a value on stock which has no formal market. It is also a way for founders to sell their stock. Since the ESOP usually creates widespread stock ownership among employees, it is viewed as a positive motivational device as well.

The Management Buyout. Founders can also realize a gain from the business by selling it to existing partners or other key managers. However, unless the buyers have the cash up front—which is rarely the case—such a sale can be fragile. Such buyouts typically require the seller to take a small amount of cash up front and a note for the balance of the purchase price over several years. The buying entrepreneurs want to stretch this as long as is possible, while the seller wants it earlier rather than later.

If the purchase price is linked to the future profitability of the business, the seller is totally dependent on the ability and integrity of the buyers. Under such an arrangement one way to lower the purchase price is to grow the business as fast as possible, spending on new products and people, and showing very little profit along the way. In five years the marginally profitable business is acquired at a bargain price, yet is positioned for excellent earnings in the next two or three years. This is one of several reasons why most advisors tell selling entrepreneurs to get the cash price up front.

The Merger. Merging two companies with complementary needs and assets is another way to realize a harvest.

Two entrepreneurs had developed some high-quality training programs for the rapidly emerging personal computer industry. Their backgrounds were in computers, rather than in marketing or general management, and they had major gaps as an entrepreneurial team. Their results in the first five years of their existence reflected this as well. Sales were under $500,000, they tended to develop custom programs only, and did no marketing. They were unable to attract any venture capital investors, even during the hot market of 1982.

Another $15 million firm had an excellent reputation for its management training programs, a Fortune-1000 customer base with an over 70% re-buy rate, and requests from the field sales force for programs to train managers to use per-

sonal computers. The marriage was consummated within about six months from the initial meeting between the founders of the two firms.

The buyer obtained 80% of the shares of the smaller firm in order to consolidate the revenues and earnings from the merged company into its own financial statements. The two founders of the smaller firm retained a 20% ownership in their firm. They also had employment contracts, and are now treated like other officers in the parent company.

The buyer provided nearly $1.5 million of capital advances during the first year of the new business; a "put" will enable the founders to realize a gain on their 20% depending upon performance of the venture over the next few years. The two founders are now reporting to the president of the parent firm, and one founder of the parent firm has taken a key executive position with them.

The Outright Sale. Most advisors to entrepreneurs attempting to harvest their venture insist that the outright sale is the ideal way to go. Cash up front is preferred over stock, even though the latter can result in a tax-free exchange. The problem is, of course, the volatility and unpredictability of the stock price of the purchasing company. Many an entrepreneur has been left with a fraction of the original purchase price when the stock price of the buyer's company declined. This lesson was driven home once again to an entirely new generation of entrepreneurial optimists on October 19, 1987! Often the acquiring company wants to lock key management into employment contracts for up to several years. Whether this makes sense depends on the goals and circumstances of the individual entrepreneur.

The Public Offering. Probably the most sacred "cow" of all is to take a company public. The vision of having one's venture listed on the stock exchanges, even over the counter, arouses all the passions of greed, glory and greatness. For many would-be entrepreneurs this aspiration is unquestioned, and enormously appealing. Yet, for all but a chosen few, taking a company public, and then living with it, may be far more trouble—and expense—than it is worth.[1]

1 See "Why I Don't Go Public," *INC.*, Nov. 1986, for a founder-CEO's perspective on this issue.

Even in the hottest new issues markets in the past twenty-five years a relatively few number of companies have gone public. A fraction of these were new or very young ventures. During the 1980s about 400 to 600 small companies went public each year, including about one third of those firms backed by venture capital. This a tiny fraction of the 600,000 to 700,000 new corporations that were formed each year during this period. Of course, the Lotus, Compaq and Apple Computers of the world do get unprecedented attention and fanfare. But these firms are truly exceptions to the rule.

What are the realities of going public, for many smaller firms? It can be a very expensive and time-consuming proposition. The following highlights of the prerequisites for an IPO give you a good profile of what it takes to go public, and what it costs. As a rule of thumb, young, dynamic, rapid-growth firms (30–50% per year) with sales of at least $10 million, and $1 million in after-tax earnings, are candidates. Most prospects have sales in the $15–20 million range with the potential to reach $50–100 million. (In very hot IPO markets, like 1983, the criteria are much broader and softer.) Established small firms with stable earnings are also candidates.

Needed are outside professional advisors, including legal and Big Eight accounting advisors, who know the ropes, i.e., have taken several to many small firms public. The cost may range from a low of 10% of the offering to as high as 30%, with 10–15% being common. Out-of-pocket expenses for all the legal, accounting, SEC and state compliance, underwriter commissions and printing costs usually run $200–350,000 or more. What is often overlooked is the post-IPO cost of being a public company: this can run $100–200,000 a year, plus a month or more of management time. In recent years, the London (England) Unlisted Securities Market (USM) and the Vancouver (Canada) market have been good alternatives.

By and large, there is no set formula for the stock price. As a guide, 500,000 to 1 million shares are sold in the $10–20 price range. Depending on market conditions at the time, this can vary considerably. The time taken to do all this? Allow six months or more from your first thoughts and "testing the waters" with advisors, to the closing. Most underwriters lay out a 120 day timetable from the first "all hands" meeting until the closing.[2]

And just because a stock is listed does not mean the founders can realize a gain. SEC restrictions on the timing and amount of stock which officers, directors and insiders can dispose of on the public market are increasingly severe. As a result it can take several years after an initial public offering before a harvest is possible.

Crafting a Harvest Strategy

A consistent pattern characterizes entrepreneurs and the harvest issue, which George Bernard Shaw understood best of all when he said, "Any damned fool can start a love affair, but it takes a real genius to end one successfully!" First, when the company is launched, struggles for survival, and begins its ascent, usually the farthest thing from the founder's mind is selling out. Psychologically this is equivalent to complete abandonment of his or her very own "baby." The intense feeling of parentage, personal involvement and identity can be as strongly felt with an entrepreneur's new venture as with a new family. (Some real children will argue even more so!)

Time and again, the founder does not even consider selling out—especially when things are finally going well—until experiencing the terror of possibly losing the company. This usually comes in an unexpected way: A new technology threatens to leap-frog completely over the current product line. A large competitor suddenly appears in a market the company thought it had to itself. A major account is lost, and the reasons elude the current management team. Panic grips the founders and shareholders of the closely-held firm, and the company is suddenly for sale: at the wrong time, for the wrong reasons and for the wrong price. What can be done about all this?

Do not panic as a result of precipitous events. Selling under duress is usually the worst of all worlds.

---

2 A complete list of underwriters is published in *Corporate Finance* magazine. Available from some Big Eight accounting firms is a guidebook, such as Ernst & Young's excellent publication, *Deciding to Go Public*.

If impatience is the enemy of an attractive harvest, greed is its executioner. Take, for example, an excellent small firm in New England, nearly eighty years old, with the third generation of successful family leadership at the helm.

Profitable growth had attracted a number of prospective acquirers, and a bona fide offer for over $25 million was made after discussion with one suitor. The owners became convinced that this "great little company" was worth considerably more; they held out. Before long, there were no buyers; market circumstances changed unfavorably, coupled with skyrocketing interest rates. Then things got worse. Soon thereafter, the company collapsed financially, ending up in bankruptcy.

Craft a harvest strategy over a period of time, at least three to five years, and as long as seven to ten. While each industry and venture within it is unique, this horizon of patience also fits with the "lemons and plums" time frame for launching and building a company that experienced venture capital investors understand.

Advisors with a "harvest mindset" are in very short supply—so start looking well before you think you will need harvest advice. It is extremely difficult to find someone to help you craft a harvest strategy while you are growing the business, and to maintain both objectivity about its value and the patience and skill to maximize it. People who sell businesses—investment bankers or business brokers—are performing the same economic role and function as real-estate brokers. Their incentive is the commission on the deal, and they want it quickly, usually within a matter of months. Contrast this with an advisor who works with the lead entrepreneur for five years or more, helping to shape and implement strategy for the whole business, so that it is positioned in the most favorable way to spot and to respond to harvest opportunities when they appear.

One good example of this is a company called HTC, Inc., a leading edge innovator in developing vapor-phase technology for soldering printed circuit boards. When advisor Joel R. Pitlor began working with this company, it was basically a one-

person, garage shop venture, with no marketable product as yet. The best the founder could do in raising venture capital was $10,000 for ten percent, from a firm that was reluctant to invest a dime. Pitlor worked closely with the lead entrepreneur so that he knew the intricacies of the market, the industry, the competitors, the customers and the internal management capabilities as the firm grew to nearly $7 million in sales. Judging by the recent sale of the company for $15 million in cash to a larger firm, their patience, positioning and involvement paid off.

Some Sobering Harvest Lessons

Here are a few of the lessons and insights that entrepreneurs say are the most difficult to acquire in their journey to a harvest, and that students and would-be entrepreneurs often lack or underestimate.

As Ye Sow ... . Clearly, harvesting is not an issue until something begins to sprout—and most start-from-scratch entrepreneurs agree that securing customers and generating continuing sales revenue is much harder and takes much longer than even they could have imagined. There is a vast difference between the existing revenue stream of an on-going business, and creating revenue where none exists. Further, the ease with which those revenue estimates can be cast and manipulated on an electronic spreadsheet belie the time and effort necessary to turn those projections into real cash.

So, while I counsel the inclusion of a harvest strategy in the long-range planning process, I emphatically emphasize that all your entrepreneurial efforts in the start-up years be directed to getting those seeds planted, and showing some healthy sprouts, before taking the time to deal with how best they can be harvested.

Adding Strategic Value. Harvests by entrepreneurs I have known, and harvests I have participated in, have three critical characteristics: First, the highest price for a company will most likely be paid a buyer with a vital strategic reason for acquiring it—technology, distribution, product line additions, key people and know-how, etc. Second, timing is invariably critical. Third, an egotistical belief that you can always get a higher price can be disastrous. Heed the advice of Bernard Baruch on this, who insisted, "I made all my money by selling too early!"

Commitment and Personal Trade-offs. There is an enormous gap between reading about it, talking about it, listening about it and doing it. The immersion, workload, sacrifices for your family, and the wear-and-tear and often the burnout experienced by entrepreneurs is real.

For instance, one computer software entrepreneur has been very successful. Working alone for several years he has developed highly sophisticated software for the banking industry. In the mid-1980s he was closing in on a harvest through the sale of his venture to a major financial institution. Yet, he is the first one to insist that he cannot stand the computer business for another day. He says he is sick of it, nearly burned out from the cumulative exhaustion of nearly fifteen years in the business. He will do almost anything to get out. This burnout may have been a significant cause of his failure to close in for the kill and actually realize some value for his efforts. He abruptly changed product lines and strategy, raised nearly $2 million from private investors, and plunged ahead. A year and a half later, the new company nearly failed before being acquired for a fraction of the invested capital.

Imagine trying to position your company for sale effectively and to negotiate a deal for a premium price when your emotional and physical fatigue have created such mental sea-anchors. If you were the buyer, would you detect his frailty, and thus negotiate a bargain price?

Some entrepreneurs, even with what most of us would agree has been raging success, wonder if the price of victory is too high. One very successful entrepreneur put it this way, "What difference does is make if you win, have $20 million in the bank—I know several who do—and you are a basket case, your family has been washed out, and your kids are a wreck?"

No Instant Winners. If you believe the popular press and government statistics there are more millionaires than ever in America. By 1990 nearly two million people in the U. S. will be millionaires—their net worth will exceed $1 million—over one and a half percent of the working population.

There are two serious flaws with these impressive numbers. To begin with, a million dollars, sadly, is not really all that much today, as a result of high rates of inflation. To illustrate, the popular TV show of the 1950s and 1960s, "The Millionaire," in which John Beresford Tipton routinely gave to astounded recipients a check for $1 million, today would have to be renamed "The Four Millionaire," merely to keep up with inflation.

The second flaw is that lottery and Irish sweepstakes winners become instant millionaires, but entrepreneurs do not. The number of years it usually takes to accumulate such a net worth is a far cry from the instant millionaire, get-rich-quick-and-easy impression associated with lottery winners or fantasy TV writers. For the vast majority of entrepreneurs it takes ten, fifteen, even twenty years or more to build a significant net worth. Doing so is neither quick nor painless.

Beyond the Harvest

You can't take it with you. The majority of highly successful entrepreneurs seem to accept a responsibility to renew and perpetuate that very system that has treated them so well.

Consider the sources of college endowments and income from gifts. Over half of the endowment at MIT has come from gifts of stock and other assets made by the founders of companies. Among the most generous and enthusiastic contributors to the Harvard Business School are the graduates of the Owner President Management Program, a short, non-degree course for the heads of smaller firms. The same pattern is also true among HBS alumni: entrepreneurs lead the way. Around the nation, a similar pattern is found: a much larger percentage of entrepreneurs, compared to their classmates, give money to their college, give more frequently and give by far the largest amounts. Even my own undergraduate alma mater—Colgate University, a liberal-arts school—has discovered the generosity of alumni who are entrepreneurs.

Entrepreneurs who have harvested very often heavily reinvest their leadership skills and money into a wide variety of civic and community activities. These range from the symphony orchestra, to museums, and to local colleges and universities. Post-harvest entrepreneurs lead fund-raising campaigns, serve on boards, and devote many hours to other voluntary work.

A young Swedish couple, after spending a six-month apprenticeship with venture capital firms in Silicon Valley and New York, was astounded at the extent to which these entrepreneurs and venture capitalists engage in such voluntary, civic activities, in sharp contrast to the Swedish pattern of paid government bureaucrats performing many of the same services.

Successful post-harvest entrepreneurs also reinvest their efforts and resources in the next generation of entrepreneurs and opportunities. They are keenly aware that the continuing existence of the U.S. system of opportunity and mobility depends in large part upon this self-renewal process. Most of them do not have a "take the money and run and hide it in a Swiss bank account" mentality.

What motivates successful entrepreneurs to behave this way? They know that perpetuating the system is far too important, and too fragile, to be left to anyone else. They have learned the hard lessons. Innovation, job creation, economic renewal are all results of the entrepreneurial process.

Appendix
Business Plan Guide

131

C. Fixed, Variable and Semi-variable Costs
D. Months to Breakeven
E. Months to Reach Positive Cash Flow

V. Marketing Plan
A. Overall Marketing Strategy
B. Pricing
C. Sales Tactics
D. Service and Warranty Policies
E. Advertising and Promotion
F. Distribution

VI. Design and Development Plans
A. Development Status and Tasks
B. Difficulties and Risks
C. Product Improvement and New Products
D. Costs
E. Proprietary Issues

VII. Manufacturing and Operations Plan
A. Geographical Location
B. Facilities and Capacity Improvements
C. Strategy and Plans
D. Regulatory, Other Compliance, Approvals and Environmental
    Issues

VIII. Management Team
A. Organization
B. Key Management Personnel
C. Management Compensation and Ownership
D. Other Investors
E. Incentives, Vesting, Employment Agreements
F. Board of Directors
G. Other Shareholders, Rights and Restrictions
H. Supporting Professional Advisors and Services

IX. Overall Schedule

X. Critical Risks and Problems

XI. The Financial Plan
A. Profit and Loss Forecasts
B. Pro Forma Cash Flow Analysis
C. Pro Forma Balance Sheets
D. Breakeven Chart and Calculation

XII. Proposed Company Offering
A. Desired Financing
B. Securities Offering
C. Capitalization
D. Use of Funds

XIII. Financial Exhibits
Exhibit 1. Pro Forma Income Statement
Exhibit 2. Pro Forma Cash Flows
Exhibit 3. Pro Forma Balance Sheets
Exhibit 4. Breakeven chart and calculation

XIV. Appendices (Could include such items as)
A. Lists, specs, pictures of products, systems, software
B. List of customers, suppliers, references
C. Appropriate location factors, facilities or technical analyses
D. Independent reports by technical expert, consultants
E. Detailed resumes of founders, key managers
F. Any critical regulatory, environmental or other compliances, licenses or approvals

Cover Page

Name of Company
Address
Telephone Number
Date
Securities Offered

This business plan has been submitted on a confidential basis solely for the benefit of selected, highly qualified investors in connection with the private placement of the above securities and is not for use by any other persons, nor may it be reproduced. By accepting delivery of this plan, the recipient agrees to return this copy to the Corporation at the address listed above if the recipient does not undertake to subscribe to the offering.

I. EXECUTIVE SUMMARY

The principal focus here is to articulate clearly the opportunity conditions, why they exist, who will execute the opportunity and why they are capable of doing so, and how the firm will gain entry and rapid market penetration. Many investors like to read a one to two page summary that highlights important features, the founders, and opportunities, in order to determine quickly whether or not the venture described is of interest.

The executive summary should be prepared last. As you draft each of the other sections note the one or two sentences, and key facts and numbers, that concisely state your key points.

Leave plenty of time to prepare an appealing, succinct and convincing summary. Really successful public speakers have been known to spend one hour of preparation for each minute of their speech. Remember that the summary is the first thing about you and your venture that a would-be investor, banker or key manager is going to read, so unless it is appealing and compelling, it will also be the last. You may have spent many weeks on the rest of your plan and it may be very good. However, if the quality does not come through in your summary, you may not get a chance to make a presentation in person at which you can respond to the difficult questions and clarify misunderstandings or misconceptions.

Your summary should contain brief statements (a paragraph or two) covering the following features of your venture:

A. <u>Summary Description of the Business</u>. You should indicate when the company was formed, what it will do, and what is special or unique about its product, service or technology. Identify any proprietary technology, trade secrets or unique capabilities that give you an edge in the marketplace. If the company has existed for a few years, give a brief summary of its size and progress.

B. <u>The Opportunity and Strategy</u>. This is the most important summary of what the opportunity is, why it is compelling, and the entry strategy that articulates how you plan to exploit the opportunity and gain rapid market acceptance and penetration. It may be presented in "bullets" of key facts, conditions, competitor vulnerabilities, industry trends and other evidence and logic that adds up to the opportunity. Note any plans for growth and expansion beyond the entry products or services.

C. The Target Market and Projections. Identify and briefly explain the market opportunity, who the primary customer groups are and how you plan to reach them. Include information on the size and growth rate for the market segments or niches you are seeking, your unit and dollar sales estimates, your anticipated market share, and your pricing position. A brief summary of industry-wide trends is also useful.

D. Competitive Advantages. Indicate the signficant competitive edges you currently enjoy, or can create, as a result of your innovative products, services and strategies, competitors' weaknesses and vulnerabilities, and any other industry conditions.

E. The Economics, Profitability and Harvest Potential. Summarize the nature of the "forgiving and rewarding economics" of the venture: gross and operating margins, expected profitability and how durable the profits appear to be; the relevant time frames to attain breakeven and positive cash flow; and the expected return on investment. Include key numbers whenever possible.

F. The Team. Summarize the relevant experience of the lead entrepreneur and any team members, noting previous profit and loss, general management, and people management experience. Include numbers that show the size of a division, a project, or prior business you ran.

G. The Offering. Briefly indicate the dollar amount of equity and/or debt financing you want, how much of your company you are prepared to offer for that financing, and what principal use will be made of the capital.

II. THE INDUSTRY, THE COMPANY AND PRODUCTS OR SERVICES

The purpose of this section is to give the investor some context for all that you are about to tell him concerning your product and its market. The section should clearly present the business that you are or will be in, the product you will offer, the nature of your industry and the opportunities available to exploit your product.

A. <u>The Industry</u>. Present the current status and prospects for the industry in which the proposed business will operate. Discuss any new products or developments, new markets and customers, new requirements, new companies and any other national or economic trends and factors that could affect the venture's business positively or negatively. Identify the source of all information used to describe industry trends.

B. <u>The Company</u>. Describe briefly what business area your company is in, or intends to enter, what products or service it will offer and who are or will be its principal customers.

By way of background, give the date your venture was incorporated, and describe the identification and development of its products and the involvement of the company's principals in that development.

If your company has been in business for several years and is seeking expansion financing, review its history and cite its prior sales and profit performance. If your company has had setbacks or losses in prior years, discuss them and emphasize what has and will be done to prevent a recurrence and improve the company's performance.

C. <u>The Products or Services</u>. The potential investor will be vitally interested in exactly what you are going to sell, what kind of product protection you have and the opportunities and possible drawbacks to your product or service.

1. <u>Description</u>. Describe in detail the products or services to be sold. Discuss the application of your product or service. Describe the primary end-use as well as any significant secondary applications. Emphasize

any unique features of your product or service, and highlight any differences between what is currently on the market and what you will offer that will account for your market penetration.

Define the present state of development of the product or service. For products, provide a summary of the functional specifications. Include photographs when available.

2. <u>Proprietary Position</u>. Describe any patents, trade secrets, or other proprietary features. Discuss any head start that you have that would enable you to achieve a favored or entrenched position in your industry.

3. <u>Potential</u>. Describe any features of your product or service that give it an advantage over the competition. Discuss any opportunities for the expansion of the product line or the development of related products or services. Emphasize your opportunities and explain how you will take advantage of them.

4. <u>Entry and Growth Strategy</u>. The entry strategy is derived from what the opportunity is asking for: how to gain a foothold in the marketplace and secure rapid market penetration. The strategy will also derive from your competitive advantages, and any weaknesses among competitors you can exploit, such as their lack of innovation, slow response time, full capacity, etc. Indicate key success variables in your marketing plan (e.g., an innovative product or marketing approach), your pricing, distribution, advertising and promotion plans. Summarize how fast you intend to grow, to what size in the first five years, and your growth plans beyond your initial products or services.

III. MARKET RESEARCH AND ANALYSIS

The purpose of this section of the plan is to present enough facts to convince the investor-reader that your venture's product or service has a substantial market in a growing industry and can achieve sales in the face of the competition. The discussion and the guidelines given below should help you do this.

This section of the business plan is one of the most difficult to prepare, and yet it is one of the most important. Almost all subsequent sections of the business plan depend on the sales estimates that are developed in this section. The sales levels predicted by the market research and analysis directly influence the size of the manufacturing operation, the marketing plan and the amount of debt and equity capital you will require. Yet most entrepreneurs seem to have great difficulty preparing and presenting market research and analyses that will convince investors that the venture's sales estimates are attainable.

Because of the importance of market analysis and the critical dependence of other parts of the plan on the sales projections, we generally advise entrepreneurs to prepare this section of the business plan before they do any other. We also advise entrepreneurs to take enough time to do this section very well and to check alternate sources of market data (consult *The Insider's Guide to Small Business Resources*, Gumpert and Timmons) for key numbers such as "market size" and "market growth rates."

A. <u>Customers</u>. Discuss who are the customers for the anticipated application of the product or service. Classify potential customers into relatively homogeneous groups (major market segment) having common, identifiable characteristics. For example, an automotive part might be sold to manufacturers and to parts distributors supplying the replacement market.

Who and where are the major purchasers for the product or service in each market segment? What are the bases of their purchase decisions: price, quality, service, personal contacts, political pressures?

List any potential customers who have expressed an interest in the product or service and indicate why. List any potential customers who have shown no interest in the proposed product or service and explain why this is so. Explain what you will do to overcome negative customer reaction. If you have an existing business, list your principal current customers and discuss the trends in your sales to them.

B. <u>Market Size and Trends</u>. What is the size of the current total market for the product or service offered? This market size should be determined from available market data sources, and from a knowledge of the purchases of competing products by potential customers in each major market segment. Discussions with potential distributors, dealers, sales representatives, and customers can be particularly useful in establishing market size and trends. Describe the size of the total market in both units and dollars. If you intend to sell regionally, show the regional market size. Indicate the sources of data and methods used to establish current market size. State also the credentials of people doing market research.

Describe the potential annual growth of the total market for your product or service for each major customer group. Total market projections should be made for at least three years. Discuss the major factors affecting market growth (industry trends, socioeconomic trends, government policy, population shifts) and review previous trends of the market. Any differences between past and projected annual growth rates should be explained. Indicate the sources of all data and methods used to make projections.

C. Competition. Make a realistic assessment of the strengths and weaknesses of competitive products and services and name the companies that supply them. State the data sources used to determine the products and the strengths of the competition.

Compare competing products or services on the basis of price, performance, service, warranties and other pertinent features. A table can be an effective way of presenting these data. Present a short discussion of the current advantages and disadvantages of competing products and services and say why they are not meeting customer needs. Indicate any knowledge of competitors' actions that could lead you to new or improved products and an advantageous position.

Review the strengths and weaknesses of the competing companies. Determine and discuss the share of the market of each competitor—the company, and its sales, distribution, and production capabilities. Review also the profitability and profit trend of the competition.

Who is the pricing leader? quality leader? Discuss why any companies have entered or dropped out of the market in recent years.

Discuss your three or four key competitors and why the customer buys from them. From what you know about their operations, explain why you think that you can capture a share of their business. Discuss what makes you think it will be easy or difficult to compete with them.

D. Estimated Market Share and Sales. Summarize what it is about your product or service that will make it salable in the face of current and potential competition.

Identify any major customers who are willing to make purchase commitments. Indicate the extent of those commitments and why they were made. Discuss which customers could be major purchasers in future years and why.

Based on your assessment of the advantages of your product or service, the market size and trends, customers, the competition and their products and the trends of sales in prior years, estimate the share of the market and the sales in units and dollars that you will acquire in each of the next three years. The growth of the company sales in units and its estimated market share should be related to the growth of its industry and customers and the strengths and weaknesses of competitors. The data can best be presented in tabular form as shown below. The assumptions used to estimate market share and sales should be clearly stated. If yours is an existing business, also indicate the total market, your market share and your sales for two prior years.

Sales and Market Share Data

		1st Year				Year	
		1Q	2Q	3Q	4Q	2	3
Estimated	Units						
total market	Dollars						
Estimated	Units						
market share, %	Dollars						
Estimated	Units						
sales	Dollars						

E. On-going Market Evaluation. Explain how you will continue to evaluate your target markets to assess customer needs and guide product-improvement programs and new-product programs, plan for expansions of your production facility, and guide product/service pricing.

IV. THE ECONOMICS OF THE BUSINESS

This section summarizes the economic and financial characteristics of the business. It should convey the fundamental attractiveness of the opportunity, including the magnitude and durability of margins and profits.

A. <u>Gross and Operating Margins</u>. Describe the magnitude of the gross margins (selling price less variable costs) and operating margins for the products and/or services you are selling. A table can effectively present such data, especially if there are several different products. Reference the appropriate exhibit for details.

B. <u>Profit Potential and Durability</u>. Describe the magnitude and expected durability of the profit stream the business will generate. Reference appropriate industry benchmarks, other competitive intelligence, or your own relevant experience. Address the issue of how perishable or durable the profit stream appears to be, and why, such as barriers to entry you can create, your technological and market lead time, etc. Indicate where the appropriate exhibits can be found in the plan, e.g., Exhibit 1, *pro forma* income statement.

C. <u>Fixed, Variable and Semi-variable Costs</u>. Provide a detailed summary of these relevant costs, in dollars and percentages as appropriate, for the various products or services you offer. A table can be a useful way to summarize them, showing the relevant industry benchmarks and sources of your estimates. Reference the appropriate exhibits in the plan, e.g., Exhibit 1.

D. <u>Months to Breakeven</u>. Given your entry strategy, marketing plan, and proposed financing, how long will it take to reach a breakeven sales level? Reference your breakeven chart and calculation in Exhibit 2. Note any significant stepwise changes in your breakeven that will occur as you grow, and add substantial capacity. This is often overlooked, along with the delays, learning curves and erosion of margins that accompany the opening of a new facility, etc.

E. Months to Reach Positive Cash Flow. Given the above strategy and assumptions, when will the venture attain a positive cash flow? When will you run out of cash? Reference your cash flow analyses in Exhibit 3, and note where the detailed assumptions can be found. Be alert to the points made in D about any stepwise changes that may affect the economics and cash flow of the venture.

V. MARKETING PLAN

The marketing plan describes how the sales projections will be attained. The marketing plan should detail the overall marketing strategy, sales and service policies, pricing, distribution and advertising strategies that will be used to achieve the estimated market share and sales projections. The marketing plan should describe *what* is to be done, *how* it will be done, and *who* will do it.

A. Overall Marketing Strategy. Describe the general marketing philosophy and strategy of the company that develops from the market research and evaluation. What kinds of customer groups will be targeted for initial intensive selling effort? What customer groups for later selling efforts? How will specific potential customers in these groups be identified and how will they be contacted? What features of the product or service—e.g., quality, price, delivery, warranty—will be emphasized to generate sales? Are there any innovative or unusual marketing concepts that will enhance customer acceptance—e.g., leasing where only sales were attempted?

Indicate whether the product or service will be introduced nationally or on a regional level. If on a regional basis, explain why and indicate any plans for extending sales to other sections of the country. Discuss any seasonal trends and what can be done to promote sales out of season.

Describe any plans to obtain government contracts as a means of supporting product development costs and overhead.

B. Pricing. Many entrepreneurs say that they have a superior product that they plan to sell for less than their competitors do. This makes a bad impression on prospective investors, for two reasons. First, if their product is as good as they say it is, they must think they are very poor salespeople to have to offer it at a lower price than the competition. Second, costs tend to be underestimated. If you start out with low costs and prices, there is little room to maneuver. Price hikes are tougher to realize than price cuts.

Pricing is one of the more important decisions you will have to make. The price must be right to penetrate the market, maintain a market position and produce profits. Devote ample time to considering a number of pricing strategies and convincingly present the one you select.

Discuss the prices to be charged for your product and service and compare your pricing policy with those of your major competitors. Discuss the gross profit margin between manufacturing and ultimate sales costs. Indicate whether this margin is large enough to allow for distribution and sales, warranty, service, amortization of development and equipment costs, price competition—and still allow you a profit.

Explain how the price you set will enable you to:
1. Get the product or service accepted.
2. Maintain and desirably increase your market share in the face of competition.
3. Produce profits.

Justify any price increases over competitive items on the basis of newness, quality, warranty and service.

If your product is to be priced lower than your competition's, explain how you will do this and maintain profitability—e.g., greater effectiveness in manufacturing and distributing the product, lower labor costs, lower overhead or lower material costs.

Discuss the relationship of price, market share and profits. For example, a higher price may reduce volume but result in a higher gross profit. Describe any discount allowance for prompt payment or volume purchases.

C. Sales Tactics. Describe the methods that will be used to make sales and distribute the product or service. Will the company use its own sales force, sales representatives, distributors? Are there ready-made manufacturers' sales organizations already selling related products that can be used? Describe both the initial plans and longer-range plans for a sales force. Discuss the margins to be given to retailers, wholesalers, and salesmen and compare them to those given by your competition.

If distributors or sales representatives are to be used, describe how they have been selected, when they will start to represent you, and the areas they will cover. Show a table that indicates the build-up of dealers and representatives by month and the expected sales to be made by each dealer. Describe any special policies regarding discounts, exclusive distribution rights, etc.

If a direct sales force is to be used, indicate how it will be structured and at what rate it will be built up. If it is to replace a dealer or representative organization, indicate when and how. Show the sales expected per salesman per year, and what commission incentive and/or salary they are slated to receive, and compare these figures to the average for your industry.

Present as an exhibit a selling schedule and a sales budget that includes all marketing , promotion and service costs.

D. Service and Warranty Policies. If your company will offer a product that will require service and warranties, indicate the importance of these to the customers' purchasing decisions and discuss your method of handling service problems. Describe the kind and term of any warranties to be offered, whether service will be handled by company servicemen, or agencies, or dealers and distributors, or factory-return. Indicate the proposed charge for service calls and whether service will be a profitable or breakeven operation. Compare your service and warranty policies and practices to those of your principal competitors.

E. Advertising and Promotion. Describe the approaches the company will use to bring its product to the attention of prospective purchasers. For original equipment manufacturer and industrial products indicate the plans for trade show participation, trade magazine advertisements, direct mailings, the preparation of product sheets and promotional literature, and use of advertising agencies. For consumer products indicate what kind of advertising and promotional campaign is contemplated to introduce the product and what kind of sales aids will be provided to dealers. The schedule and cost of promotion and advertising should be presented. If advertising will be a significant part of company expenses, an exhibit showing how and when these costs will be incurred should be included.

F. <u>Distribution</u>. Describe the methods and channels of distribution you will employ. How sensitive is shipping cost as a percent of the selling price? Note any special issues or problems that need to be resolved, or present potential vulnerabilities. Provide any tables or exhibits that can show the facts that are pertinent here.

VI. DESIGN AND DEVELOPMENT PLANS

If the product, process or service of the proposed venture requires any design and development before it is ready to be placed on the market, the nature and extent of this work should be fully discussed. The investor will want to know the extent and nature of any design and development and the costs and time required to achieve a marketable product. Such design and development might be the engineering work necessary to convert a laboratory prototype to a finished product, or the design of special tooling, or the work of an industrial designer to make a product more attractive and salable, or the identification and organization of manpower, equipment and special techniques to implement a service business—e.g., the equipment, new computer software and skills required for computerized credit checking.

A. <u>Development Status and Tasks</u>. Describe the current status of the product or service and explain what remains to be done to make it marketable. Describe briefly the competence or expertise that your company has or will acquire to complete this development.

B. <u>Difficulties and Risks</u>. Identify any major anticipated design and development problems and approaches to their solution. Discuss their possible effect on the schedule, cost of design and development and time of market introduction.

C. Product Improvement and New Products. In addition to describing the development of the initial products, discuss any ongoing design and development work that is planned to keep your product or service competitive and to develop new related products that can be sold to the same group of customers.

D. Costs. Present and discuss a design and development budget. The cost should include labor, materials, consulting fees, etc. Design and development costs are often underestimated. This can have a serious impact on cash flow projections. Accordingly, consider and perhaps show a 15% to 30% cost contingency. These cost data will become an integral part of the financial plan (See Part XI, The Financial Plan).

E. Proprietary Issues. Describe any patent, trademark or intellectual property rights that you own, or are seeking. Also note any unresolved issues relating to your proprietary rights that can bear on your timing and competitive edge. Note any other existing or possible action pending with respect to them, such as disputed rights of ownership or other such factors.

VII. MANUFACTURING AND OPERATIONS PLAN

The manufacturing and operations plan should describe the kind of facilities, plant location, space requirements, capital equipment and labor force (part- and full-time) required to provide the company's product or service. For a manufacturing business, discuss your policies on inventory control, purchasing, production control and "make or buy decisions" (i.e., which parts of the product will be purchased and which will be made by your work force). A service business may require particular attention and focus on an appropriate location, how you will minimize overhead and how you will obtain competitive productivity from your labor force.

The discussion guidelines given below are general enough to cover both product and service businesses. Only those that are relevant to your venture—be it product or service—should be addressed in the business plan.

A. <u>Geographical Location</u>. Describe the planned geographical location of the business and discuss any advantages or disadvantages of the site location in terms of wage rates, labor unionization, labor availability, closeness to customers or suppliers, access to transportation, state and local taxes and laws, utilities and zoning. For a service business, proximity to customers is generally a "must."

B. <u>Facilities and Improvements</u>. If yours is an existing business, describe the facilities currently used to conduct the company's business. This should include plant and office space, storage and land areas, machinery, special tooling and other capital equipment.

If your venture is a start-up, describe how and when the necessary facilities to start production will be acquired. Discuss whether equipment and space will be leased or acquired (new or used) and indicate the costs and timing of such actions. Indicate how much of the proposed financing will be devoted to plant and equipment. (These cost data will become part of the financial plan.)

Discuss how and when plant space and equipment will be expanded to the capacities required by future sales projections. Discuss any plans to improve or add to existing plant space or move the facility. Explain future equipment needs and indicate the timing and cost of such acquisitions. A three-year planning period should be used for these projections.

C. <u>Strategy and Plans</u>. Describe the manufacturing processes involved in your product's production and any decisions with respect to subcontracting of component parts rather than complete in-house manufacture. The "make or buy" strategy adopted should be determined by consideration of inventory financing, available labor skills and other non-technical questions, as well as purely production, cost and capability issues. Justify your proposed "make or buy" policy. Discuss any surveys of potential subcontractors and suppliers, and who they are likely to be.

Present a production plan that shows cost-volume information at various sales levels of operation, with breakdowns of applicable material, labor, purchased components and factory overhead. Discuss the inventory required at various sales levels. These data will be incorporated into cash-flow projections. Explain how any seasonal production loads will be handled without severe dislocation; e.g., by building to inventory or using part-time help in peak periods.

Briefly, describe your approach to quality control, production control, inventory control. Explain what quality-control and inspection procedures the company will use to minimize service problems and associated customer dissatisfaction.

D. Regulatory, Other Compliance, Approvals, Environmental Issues. Include here any relevant regulatory requirements unique to your product, process or service. What approvals are necessary in order to begin operation, such as permits, licenses, zoning, health, environmental and the like? What laws or other regulatory compliance are necessary and unique to your business? Note any pending regulatory changes that can affect the nature and timing window on your opportunity, such as occurred in airline deregulation, and in the AT&T break-up. Are there any legal or contractual obligations that are pertinent as well?

VIII. MANAGEMENT TEAM

The management team is the key to turning a good idea into a successful business. Investors look for a committed management team with a proper balance of technical, managerial and business skills, and experience in doing what is proposed.

Accordingly, this section of the business plan will be of primary interest to potential investors and will significantly influence their investment decisions. It should include a description of the key management personnel and their primary duties, the organizational structure and the board of directors.

A. <u>Organization</u>. Present in tabular form the key management roles in the company and the individual who will fill each position.

Discuss any current or past situations where the key management people have worked together that indicate how their skills complement each other and result in an effective management team. If any key individuals will not be on board at the start of the venture, indicate when they will join the company.

In a new business, it may not be possible to fill each executive role with a full-time person without excessively burdening the overhead of the venture. One solution is to use part-time specialists or consultants to perform some functions. If this is your plan, discuss it and indicate who will be used and when they will be replaced by a full-time staff member.

If the company is established and of sufficient size, an organization chart can be appended as an exhibit.

B. <u>Key Management Personnel</u>. Describe the exact duties and responsibilities of each of the key members of the management team. Include a brief (three- or four-sentence) statement of the career highlights of each individual that focuses on accomplishments that demonstrates his or her ability to perform the assigned role.

Complete resumes for each key management member should be included here or as an exhibit to the business plan. These resumes should stress the training, experience and accomplishments of each manager in performing functions similar to the new role in the venture. Accomplishments should be discussed in concrete terms, such as profit and sales improvement, labor management, manufacturing or technical achievements and ability to meet budgets and schedules.

C. <u>Management Compensation and Ownership</u>. The likelihood of obtaining financing for a start-up is small when the founding management team is not prepared to accept initial modest salaries. If the founders demand substantial salaries, in excess of what they received at their prior employment, the potential investor will conclude that their psychological commitment to the venture is a good deal less than it should be.

State the salary that is to be paid to each key person and compare it to the salary received at his last independent job. Set forth the stock ownership planned for the key personnel, the amount of their equity investment (if any), and any performance-dependent stock option or bonus plans that are contemplated.

D. <u>Other Investors</u>. Describe here any other investors in your venture, the number and percent of outstanding shares they owned, when they were acquired, and at what price.

E. <u>Incentives, Vesting, Employment Agreements</u>. Summarize here any incentive stock option (ISO) or other stock ownership plans you have in effect, or plan to have for key people and employees. Note restrictions on stock and any vesting or other agreements that affect its ownership and disposition, and any employment agreements that exist or are contemplated. Eventually, the investor will want to review copies of these documents.

F. <u>Board of Directors</u>. Discuss the company's philosophy as to the size and composition of the board. Identify any proposed board members, and include a one- or two-sentence statement of the member's background that shows what he or she can bring to the company.

G. <u>Other Shareholders, Rights and Restrictions</u>. Briefly summarize here any other shareholders in your company, and any rights, obligations—such as notes, guarantees—and restrictions associated with these. If they have all been accounted for above, simply note that there are no others.

H. <u>Supporting Professional Advisors and Services</u>. State the legal (including patent), accounting, advertising, and banking organizations that you have selected for your venture and—if applicable—the names and affiliations of any close advisors you have worked with. Capable, reputable, and well-known individuals and supporting service organizations can not only provide significant direct professional assistance, but can also add to the credibility of your venture. In addition, properly selected professional organizations can help you establish good contacts in the business community, identify potential investors and help you secure financing.

IX. OVERALL SCHEDULE

A schedule that shows the timing and interrelationship of the major events necessary to launch the venture and realize its objectives is an essential part of a business plan. In addition to being a planning aid and showing deadlines critical to a venture's success, a well-prepared schedule can be an extremely effective sales tool in raising money from potential investors. A well-prepared and realistic schedule demonstrates the ability of the management team to plan for venture growth in a way that recognizes obstacles and minimizes investor risk.

Prepare, as a part of this section, a month-by-month schedule that shows the timing of such activities as product development, market planning, sales programs and production and operations. Sufficient detail should be included to show the timing of the primary tasks required to accomplish an activity.

Show on the schedule the deadlines or milestones critical to the venture's success. This should include such events as:

1. Incorporation of the venture (for a new business).
2. Completion of design and development.
3. Completion of prototypes (a key date; its achievement is a tangible measure of the company's ability to perform).
4. Sales representatives are hired.
5. Product display at trade shows.
6. Distributors and dealers are signed up.
7. Ordering of materials in production quantities.
8. Start of production or operation (another key date because it is related to the production of income).
9. Receipt of first orders.
10. First sales and deliveries (a date of maximum interest because it relates directly to the company's credibility and need for capital).
11. Payment of first accounts receivable (cash in).

The schedule should also show the following and their relation to the development of the business:

1. Number of management personnel.

2. Number of production and oeprations personnel.

3. Additions to plant or equipment.

Discuss in a general way the activities most likely to cause a schedule slippage, and what steps you would take to correct such slippages. Discuss the impact of schedule slippages on the venture's operation, especially its potential viability and capital needs. Keep in mind that the time to do things tends to be underestimated—even more than financing requirements—so be realistic about your schedule.

X. CRITICAL RISKS AND PROBLEMS

The development of a business has risks and problems, and the business plan invariably contains some implicit assumptions about them. The discovery of any unstated negative factors by potential investors can undermine the credibility of the venture and endanger its financing.

On the other hand, identifying and discussing the risks in your venture demonstrates your skills as a manager and increases the credibility of you and your venture with a venture capital investor. Taking the initiative on the identification and discussion of risks helps you to demonstrate to the investor that you have thought about them and can handle them. Risks then tend not to loom as such large black clouds in the investor's thinking about your venture.

Accordingly, identify and discuss in the business plan the major problems and risks that you think you will have to deal with to develop the venture. This should include a description of the risks relating to your industry, your company and its personnel, your product's market appeal and the timing and financing of your startup. Among the risks that might require discussion are:

1. Potential price cutting by competitors.

2. Any potentially unfavorable industry-wide trends.

3. Design or manufacturing costs in excess of estimates.

4. Sales projections not achieved.

5. Product development schedule not met.

6. Difficulties or long lead times encountered in the procurement of parts or raw materials.

7. Difficulties encountered in obtaining needed bank credit line because of tight money.

8. Larger-than-expected innovation and development costs to stay competitive.

This is not meant to be complete but only indicative of the kinds of risks and assumptions that might be discussed.

Indicate which business plan assumptions or potential problems are most critical to the success of the venture. Describe your plans for minimizing the impact of unfavorable developments in each risk area on the success of your venture.

XI. THE FINANCIAL PLAN

The financial plan is basic to the evaluation of an investment opportunity and should represent the entrepreneur's best estimates of future operations—your best judgement of the results you believe are realistic and attainable. The purpose of the financial plan is to indicate the venture's potential and timetable for financial viability. It can also serve as an operating plan for financial management of the venture.

In developing the financial plan, four basic exhibits need to be prepared (see Chapter 3):

Profit and Loss Forecasts for at least the first three years. A yearly summary is also helpful.

Cash Flow Projections for the same periods. Remember, happiness is a positive cash flow.

Pro Forma Balance Sheets at start-up quarterly in the first year, and at the end of each of the first three years of operation.

Breakeven Chart and Calculation to show when breakeven will be reached, and to capture any stepwise changes in breakeven that may occur. With higher margin ventures, say over 40% to 40% or more, it is not as critical as would be in a lower margin, more price-sensitive business.

In the case of an *existing business seeking expansion capital*, income statements and balance sheets for the current and prior two years should be provided, in addition to these estimates.

After you have completed the preparation of the financial exhibits, briefly highlight in writing the important conclusions that can be drawn. These might include the maximum cash requirement and when it will be reached, when you will reach breakeven and a positive cash flow, the amount of debt and equity needed, the level of profits as a percent of sales, how fast any debts are repaid, etc.

Finally, on the appropriate exhibits, or in an attachment, specify the assumptions behind the plan, such as how you estimated sales level and growth, collections and payables periods, inventory requirements, minimum cash balance, cost of goods, and other line items comparable to industry ratios.

A. Profit and Loss Forecast (See Exhibit 1). The preparation of *pro forma* income statements is the planning-for-profit part of financial management. Crucial to the earnings forecasts—as well as other projections—is the sales forecast. The methods for developing sales forecasts are described in Section II of these guidelines, and the sales data projected should be used here.

Once the sales forecasts are in hand, production costs (or operations costs for a service business) should be budgeted. The level of production or operation that is required to meet the sales forecasts and also to fulfill inventory requirements must be determined. The material, labor, service and manufacturing overhead requirements must be developed and translated into cost data. A separation of the fixed and variable elements of these costs is desirable, and the effect of sales volume on inventory, equipment acquisitions and manufacturing costs should be taken into account.

Sales expense should include the costs of selling and distribution, storage, discounts, advertising and promotion. General and administrative expense should include management salaries, secretarial costs and legal and accounting expenses. Manufacturing or operations overhead includes rent, utilities, fringe benefits, telephone, etc.

Earnings projections should be prepared monthly in the first year of operation and quarterly for the second and third years.

If these earnings projections are to be useful they must represent management's realistic and best estimates of probable operating results. Sales or operational cost projections that are either too conservative or too optimistic have little value as aids to policy formulation and decision-making.

1. Discussion of Assumptions. Because of the importance of profit and loss projections as an indication of the financial feasibility of a new venture to potential investors, it is extremely important that any assumptions made in its preparation be fully explained and documented. Such assumptions could include the amount allowed for bad debts and discounts, and any assumptions made about sales expenses or general and administrative costs as a fixed percentage of costs or sales.

2. Risks and Sensitivity. Once the income statements have been prepared, draw on Section X of these guidelines and highlight any major risks that could prevent the venture's sales and profit goals from being attained, and the sensitivity of profits to these risks.

This discussion should reflect the entrepreneur's thinking about some of the risks that might be encountered in the firm itself, the industry, and the environment. This could include such things as the effect of a 20% reduction in sales projections, or the impact of a learning curve on the level of productivity over time.

B. _Pro Forma_ Cash Flow Analysis (See Exhibit 2). For a new venture the cash-flow forecast can be more important than the forecasts of profits because it details the amount and timing of expected cash inflows and outflows. Usually the level of profits, particularly during the start-up years of a venture, will not be sufficient to finance operating asset needs. Moreover, cash inflows do not match the outflows on a short-term basis. The cash-flow forecast will indicate these conditions and enable management to plan cash needs.

Given a level of projected sales and capital expenditures over a specific period, the cash forecast will highlight the need for and timing of additional financing and indicate peak requirements for working capital. Management must decide how this additional financing is to be obtained, on what terms, and how it is to be repaid. (Part of the needed financing may be supplied by equity financing, part by bank loans for one to five years, and the balance by short-term lines of credit from banks.) This information becomes part of the final cash-flow forecast.

If the venture is in a seasonal or cyclical industry, or is in an industry in which suppliers require a new firm to pay cash, or if an inventory buildup occurs before the product can be sold and produces revenues, the cash-flow forecast is crucial to the continuing solvency of the business. A detailed cash-flow forecast that is understood and used by management can enable them to direct their attention to operating problems without the distractions caused by periodic cash crises that should have been anticipated. Cash-flow projections should be made for each month of the first year of operation and quarterly for the second and third years.

1. Discussion of Assumptions. This should include assumptions made on the timing of collection of receivables, trade discounts given, terms of payments to vendors, planned salary and wage increases, anticipated increases in any operating expenses, seasonal characteristics of the business as they affect inventory requirements, inventory turn-overs per year, and capital equipment purchases. Thinking about such assumptions when planning your venture is useful for identifying issues that may later require attention if they are not to become significant problems.

2. Cash-Flow Sensitivity. Once the cash flow has been completed, discuss the implications for cash needs that possible changes in some of the crucial assumptions would have, e.g., an increase in the receivable collection period or sales below forecasts. This will enable you to test the sensitivity of the cash budget to a variety of assumptions about business factors and to view a wider range of possible outcomes. Investors are vitally interested in this because it helps them estimate the possibility that you will need more cash sooner than planned.

C. _Pro Forma_ Balance Sheets (See Exhibit 3). The balance sheets are used to detail the assets required to support the projected level of operations and, through liabilities, show how these assets are to be financed. Investors and bankers look to the projected balance sheets to determine if debt-to-equity ratios, working capital, current ratios, inventory turnover, etc., are within the acceptable limits required to justify future financings projected for the venture.

Pro forma balance sheets should be prepared at start-up, quarterly for the first year, and at the end of each of the first three years of operation.

D. Break-even Chart (See Exhibit 4). A break-even chart is a way of determining the level of sales and production that will cover all costs. This includes those costs that vary with production level (manufacturing labor, material, sales costs) and those that do not change with production level (rent, interest charges, executive salaries, etc.) The sales level that just covers all costs is the break-even level for your venture.

It is very useful for the investor and the management to know what the break-even point is, and whether it will be easy or difficult to attain. It is also very desirable that your projected sales be sufficiently larger than the break-even sales so that small perturbations in the venture's performance do not produce losses. You should prepare a break-even chart and discuss how your break-even point might be lowered in case you start to fall short of your sales projections.

E. Cost Control. Your ability to meet your income and cash flow projections will depend critically on your ability to monitor and control costs. For this reason many investors like to know what sort of accounting and cost control system you have or will use in your business. Accordingly, the financial plan should include a brief description of how you will obtain and report costs, who will be responsible for the control of the various cost elements, how often he or she will obtain cost data and how you will take action on budget overruns.

XII. PROPOSED COMPANY OFFERING

The purpose of this section of the plan is to indicate the amount of money that is being sought, the nature and amount of the securities offered to the investor, and a brief description of the uses that will be made of the capital raised. The discussion and guidelines given below should help you do this.

You should, however, realize that the terms for financing your company you propose are only the first step in negotiating with a capital investor interested in your deal. It is very possible that when you close your financing, you will be selling a different kind of security (e.g., convertible debt instead of common stock) for a different price than you originally proposed.

A. <u>Desired Financing</u>. Summarize from your cash-flow projections how much money is required over the first three years to carry out the development and expansion of your business that has been described. Indicate how much of this capital will be obtained by this offering and how much will be obtained via term loans and lines of credit.

B. <u>Securities Offering</u>. Describe the kind (common stock, covertible debenture, etc.), unit price and total amount of securities to be sold in this offering. If the securities are not just common stock (e.g., debt with warrants, debt plus stock), indicate interest, maturity and conversion conditions. Also show the percentage of the company investors in this offering will hold after it is completed, or after exercise of any stock conversion or purchase rights in the case of convertible debentures or warrants.

If the securities are being sold as a private placement exempt from SEC registration, you should include the following statement in this part of the plan:

"The shares being sold pursuant to this offering are restricted securities and may not be resold readily. The prospective investor should recognize that such securities might be restricted as to resale for an indefinite period of time. Each purchaser will be required to execute a Non-Distribution Agreement satisfactory in form to corporate counsel."

C. <u>Capitalization</u>. Present in tabular form the current and proposed (post-offering) number of outstanding shares of common stock. Indicate any shares offered by key management people and show the number of shares that they will hold after completion of the proposed financing.

Indicate how many shares of your company's common stock will remain authorized but unissued after the offering and how many of these will be reserved for stock options for future key employees.

D. <u>Use of Funds</u>. Investors like to know how their money is going to be spent. Provide a brief description of how the capital raised will be used. Summarize, as specifically as possible, what amount will be used for such things as product design and development, capital equipment, marketing and general working-capital needs.

XIII. FINANCIAL EXHIBITS

EXHIBIT 1 *PRO FORMA* INCOME STATEMENTS

	1st Year Months	2d Year Quarters	3d Year Quarters
Sales			
Less: Discounts			
Less: Bad debt provision			
Less: Materials used			
Direct labor			
Manufacturing overhead*			
Other manufacturing			
Expense (leases)			
Depreciation			
Gross profit or (loss)			
Less:			
Sales expense			
Engineering expense			
General and administrative expense†			
Operating profit or (loss)			
Less: Other expense (e.g., interest)			
Profit before taxes (or loss)			
Profit after taxes			

*Includes rent, utilities, fringe benefits, telephone.
†Includes office supplies, accounting and legal services, management, etc.

EXHIBIT 2 *PRO FORMA* CASH FLOWS

	1st Year Months	2d Year Quarters	3d Year Quarters
Opening cash balance			
Add cash receipts:			
Collection of accounts receivable			
Miscellaneous receipts			
Bank loan proceeds			
Sale of stock			
Total receipts			
Less disbursements:			
Trade payables			
Direct labor			
Manufacturing overhead			
Leased equipment			
Sales expense			
Warranty expense			
General administrative expense			
Fixed asset additions			
Income tax			
Loan interest @_____ %			
Loan repayments			
Other payments			
Total disbursements			
Cash increase (or decrease)			
Closing cash balance			

EXHIBIT 3 *PRO FORMA* BALANCE SHEETS

	Start-up Date quarters	lstYear annual	2d Year annual	3d Year annual

Assets

Cash
Marketable securities
Accounts receivable
Inventory:
Raw materials and supplies
Work in process
Finish goods
Total inventory
Prepaid items
Total current assets
Plant and equipment
Less: accumulated depreciation
Net plant and equipment
Deferred charges
Other assets (identify)

Total assets

Liabilities and Stockholders equity

Notes payable to bank
Accounts payable
Accruals
Federal and state taxes accrued
Other
Long-term notes
Other liabilities
Common stock
Capital surplus
Retained earnings
Stockholders' equity

Total liabilities and stockholders' equity

EXHIBIT 4 SAMPLE BREAKEVEN CHART

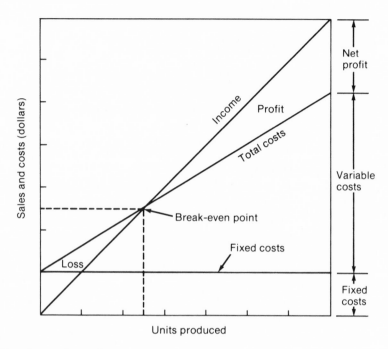

Breakeven formula:
SP = Selling price (unit)
VC = Direct or variable costs (e.g., labor, material)
FC = Fixed costs
SP-VC = Gross margin, or contribution to profit and fixed costs

Therefore,
Total fixed costs/$ contribution = Number of units required to break even.

XIV. APPENDICES

Include pertinent information here not covered elsewhere that may be unique to your venture. For instance, this could be product specs or photos, list of customers as references, or suppliers of critical components; special location factors, facilities or technical analyses, reports from consultants or technical experts, and any critical regulatory, environmental or other compliances or approvals necessary.

Appendix II
Outline of an
Investment Agreement

What follows is a detailed outline of the contents of a venture investment agreement. The main sections of a typical agreement are briefly described, and many of the terms that might appear in each section are noted. However, not all of the terms listed will appear in an investment agreement. Venture capital investors select terms from among those listed (and some not listed) to best serve their needs in a particular venture investment situation.

1. Description of the Investment

This section of the agreement defines the basic terms of the investment. It includes descriptions of the:

a. Amount and type of investment.

b. Securities to be issued.

c. Guarantees, collateral subordination and payment schedules associated with any notes.

d. Conditions of closing: time, place, method of payment.

When investment instruments are involved that carry warrants or debt conversion privileges, the agreement will completely describe them. This description will include the:

a. Time limits on the exercise of the warrant or conversion of the debt.

b. Price and any price changes that vary with the time of exercise.

c. Transferability of the instruments.

d. Registration rights on stock acquired by the investor.

e. Dilution resulting from exercise of warrants or debt conversion.

f. Rights and protections surviving after conversion, exercise, or redemption.

2. Preconditions to Closing

This section covers what the venture must do or what ancillary agreements and documents must be submitted to the investor before the investment can be closed. These agreements and documents may include:

a. Corporate documents; e.g., bylaws, articles of incorporation, resolutions authorizing sale of securities, tax status certificates, list of stockholders and directors.

b. Audited financial statements.

c. Any agreements for simultaneous additional financing from another source or for lines of credit.

d. Ancillary agreements; e.g., employment contracts, stock option agreements, key man insurance policies, stock repurchase agreements.

e. Copies of any leases or supply contracts.

3. Representations and Warranties by the Venture

This section contains legally binding statements made by the venture's officers that describe its condition on or before the closing date of the investment agreement. The venture's management will warrant:

a. That it is a duly organized corporation in good standing.

b. That its action in entering into an agreement is authorized by its directors, allowed by its bylaws and charter, legally binding upon the corporation, and not in breach of any other agreements.

c. If a private placement, that the securities being issued are exempt from registration under the Securities Act of 1933 as amended and under state securities law and that registration is not required under the Securities Exchange Act of 1934.

d. That the capitalization, shares, options, directors and shareholders of the company are as described (either in the agreement or in an exhibit).

e. That no trade secrets or patents will be used in the business that are not owned free and clear or if rights to use them have not been acquired.

f. That no conflicts of interest exist in their entering the agreement.

g. That all material facts and representations in the agreement and exhibits are true as of the date of closing (includes accuracy of business plan and financials).

h. That the venture will fulfill its part of the agreement so long as all conditions are met.

i. That any patents, trademarks or copyrights owned and/or used by the company are as described.

j. That the principal assets and liabilities of the company are as described in attached exhibits.

k. That there are no undisclosed obligations, litigations or agreements of the venture of a material nature not already known to all parties.

l. That any prior-year income statements and balance sheets are accurate as presented and have been audited and that there have been no adverse changes since the last audited statements.

m. That the venture is current on all tax payments and returns.

4. Representations and Warranties by the Investor

This section contains any legally binding representations made by the investor. They are much smaller in number than those made by the company. The investor may warrant:

a. If a corporation, that it is duly organized and in good standing.

b. If a corporation, that its action in entering into an agreement with the venture is authorized by its directors, allowed by its bylaws and charter, legally binding upon the corporation, and not in breach of any existing agreements.

c. If a private placement, that the stock being acquired is for investment and not with a view to or for sale in connection with any distribution.

d. The performance of his or her part of the contract if all conditions are met.

5. Affirmative Covenants

In addition to the above representations and warranties, the company in which the investor invests usually has a list of affirmative covenants with which it must comply. These could include agreeing to:

a. Pay taxes, fees, duties and other assessments promptly.

b. File all appropriate government or agency reports.

c. Pay debt principal and interest.

d. Maintain corporate existence.

e. Maintain appropriate books of accounts and keep a specified auditing firm on retainer.

f. Allow access to these records to all directors and representatives of the investor.

g. Provide the investor with periodic income statements and balance sheets.

h. Preserve and provide for the investor's stock registration rights as described in the agreement.

i. Maintain appropriate insurance, including key man insurance, with the company as beneficiary.

j. Maintain minimum net worth, working capital, or net asset levels.

k. Maintain the number of investor board seats prescribed in the agreement.

l. Hold the prescribed number of directors' meetings.

m. Comply with all applicable laws.

n. Maintain corporate properties in good condition.

o. Notify the investor of any events of default of the investment agreement within a prescribed time.

p. Use the investment proceeds substantially in accordance with a business plan that is an exhibit to the agreement.

6. Negative Covenants

These covenants define what a venture must not do, or must not do without prior investor approval; such approval not to be unreasonably withheld. A venture usually agrees not to do such things as:

a. Merge, consolidate with, acquire or invest in any form of organization.

b. Amend or violate the venture's charter or bylaws.

c. Distribute, sell, redeem or divide stock except as provided for in the agreement.

d. Sell, lease or dispose of assets whose value exceeds a specified amount.

e. Purchase assets whose value exceeds a specified amount.

f. Pay dividends.

g. Violate any working capital or net worth restrictions described in the investment agreement.

h. Advance to, loan to or invest in individuals, organizations or firms except as described in the investment agreement.

i. Create subsidiaries.

j. Liquidate the corporation.

k. Institute bankruptcy proceedings.

l. Pay compensation to its management other than as provided for in the agreement.

m. Change the basic nature of the business for which the firm was organized.

n. Borrow money except as provided for in the agreement.

o. Dilute the investors' holdings without giving them the right of first refusal on new issues of stock.

7. Conditions of Default

This section describes those events that constitute a breach of the investment agreement if not corrected within a specified time and under which an investor can exercise specific remedies. Events that constitute default may include:

a. Failure to comply with the affirmative or negative covenants of the investment agreement.

b. Falsification of representations and warranties made in the investment agreement.

c. Insolvency or reorganization of the venture.

d. Failure to pay interest or principal due on debentures.

8. Remedies

This section describes the actions available to an investor in the event that a condition of default occurs. Remedies depend on the form an investment takes. For a common-stock investment, the remedies could be:

a. Forfeiture to the investor of any stock of the venture's principals that was held in escrow.

b. The investor's receiving voting control through a right to vote some or all of stock of a venture's principals.

c. The right of the investor to "put" his stock to the company at a predetermined price.

For a debenture, the remedies might be:

a. The full amount of the note becoming due and payable on demand.

b. Forfeiture of any collateral used to secure the debt.

In the case of a preferred stock investment, the remedy can be special voting rights (e.g., the right to vote the entrepreneur's stock) to obtain control of the board of directors.

9. Other Conditions

A number of other clauses that cover a diverse group of issues often appear in investment agreements. Some of the more common issues covered are:

a. Who will bear the costs of closing the agreement; this is often borne by the company.

b. Who will bear the costs of registration of the investors' stocks; again, the investors prefer that this be borne by the company for the first such registration.

c. Right of first refusal for the investor on subsequent company financings.

Appendix III
Sample Terms Sheet

CURTIS-PALMER & COMPANY, INC.
Summary of Principal Terms

Amount: $_____ .

Security: _____ shares of Convertible Preferred Stock ("Preferred") at a price of $_____ per share ("Original Purchase Price").

Rights, Preferences, Privileges, and Restrictions of Preferred Stock:

1. *Dividend Provisions:* The Preferred Stock shall be entitled to dividends at the same rate as the Common Stock ("Common") (based on the number of shares of Common into which the Preferred is convertible on the date the dividend is declared).

2. *Liquidation Preference:* In the event of any liquidation of the Company, the Preferred will be entitled to receive in preference to the Common an amount equal to the Original Purchase Price.

3. *Redemption:* The Company will redeem the Preferred in three equal annual installments commencing six (6) years from the date of purchase by paying in cash a total amount equal to the Original Purchase Price.

4. *Conversion:* The Preferred will be convertible at any time, at the option of the holder, into shares of Common Stock of the Company at an initial conversion price equal to the Original Purchase Price. Initially, each share of Preferred is convertible into one share of Common Stock. The conversion price will be subject to adjustment as provided in paragraph 6 below.

5. *Automatic Conversion:* The Preferred will be automatically converted into Common, at the then applicable conversion price, in the event of an underwritten public offering of shares of Common at a price per share that is not less than five times the Original Purchase Price in an

offering resulting in gross proceeds to the Company of not less than $10 million.

6. *Antidilution Provisions:* The conversion price of the Preferred Stock will be subject to adjustment to prevent dilution n the event that the Company issues additional shares (other than the Reserved Employee Shares described under "Reserved Employee Shares" below) at a purchase price less than the applicable conversion price. The conversion price will be subject to adjustment on a weighted basis which takes into account issuances of additional shares at prices below the applicable conversion price.

7. *Voting Rights:* Except with respect to election of directors, the holder of a share of Preferred will have the right to that number of votes equal to the number of shares of Common issuable upon conversion of the Preferred at the time the record for the vote is taken. Election of directors will be as described under "Board Representation" below.

8. *Protective Provisions:* Consent of the holders of at least two thirds of the Preferred will be required for any sale by the Company of a substantial portion of its assets, any merger of the Company with another entity, each amendment of the Company's articles of incorporation, and for any action which (i) alters or changes the rights, preferences, or privileges of Preferred materially and adversely; (ii) increases the authorized number of shares of Preferred Stock; or (iii) creates any new class of shares having preference over or being on a parity with the Preferred.

Information Rights:

The company will timely furnish the Investors with annual, quarterly and monthly financial statements. Representatives of the Investors will have the right to inspect the books and records of the Company.

Registration Rights:

1. *Demand Rights:* If investors holding at least 50 percent of the Preferred (or Common issued upon conversion of the Preferred) request that the Company file a Registration Statement covering at least 20 percent of the Common issuable upon conversion of the Preferred, the Com-

pany will use its best efforts to cause such shares to be registered. The Company will not be obligated to effect more than two registrations (other than form S-3) under these demand right provisions.

2. *Registration on Form S-3:* Holders of 10 percent or more of the Preferred (or Common issued upon conversion of the Preferred) will have the right to require the Company to file an unlimited number of Registration Statements on Form S-3 (but no more than two per year).

3. *Piggyback Registration:* The Investors will be entitled to "piggyback" registration rights on all registrations of the Company.

4. *Registration Expenses:* All registration expenses (exclusive of underwriting discounts and commissions or special counsel fees of a selling shareholder) shall be borne by the Company.

Board Representation:

The Board will consists of _____ members. The holders of Preferred will have the right to designate _____ directors; the holders of the Common (exclusive of the Investors) will have the right to designate _____ directors; and the remaining _____ directors will be unaffiliated persons elected by the holders of Common and the holders of Preferred voting as a single class.

Key Man Insurance:

As determined by the Board of Directors.

Preemptive Right to Purchase New Securities:

If the Company proposes to offer additional shares (other than Reserved Employee Shares or shares issued in the acquisition of another company), the Company will first offer all such shares to the Investors on a pro rata basis. This preemptive right will terminate upon an underwritten public offering of shares of the Company.

Stock Restriction and Stockholders Agreements:

All present holders of Common Stock of the Company who are employees of, or consultants to, the Company will execute a Stock Restriction Agreement with the Company pursuant to which the Company will have an option to buy back at cost a portion of the shares of Common Stock held by such person in the event that such shareholder's employment with the Company is terminated prior to the expiration of 48 months from the date of employment; 25 percent of the shares will be released each year from the repurchase option based upon continued employment by the Company. In addition, the Company and the Investors will have a right of first refusal with respect to any employee's shares proposed to be resold or, alternatively, the right to participate in the sale of any such shares to a third party, which rights will terminate upon a public offering.

Reserved Employee Shares:
The Company may reserve up to _____ shares of Common Stock for issuance to employees of the Company (the "Reserved Employee Shares"). The Reserved Employee Shares will be issued from time to time under such arrangements, contracts, or plans as are recommended by management and approved by the Board.

Noncompetition, Proprietary Information, and Inventions Agreement:
Each officer and key employee of the Company designated by the Investors will enter into a noncompetition, proprietary information, and inventions agreement in a form reasonably acceptable to the investors.

The Purchase Agreement:
The purchase of the Preferred will be made pursuant to a Stock Purchase Agreement drafted by counsel to the Investors and reasonably acceptable to the Company and the Investors, which agreement shall contain, among other things, appropriate representations and warranties of the Company, covenants of the Company reflecting the provisions set forth herein, and appropriate conditions of closing.

Expenses:
The Company will bear the legal fees and other out-of-pocket expenses of the Investors with respect to the transaction.

Appendix IV
Sample Vesting and Stock Restriction Agreement

Agreement, dated as of January 1, 1990, between Venture X, a Massachusetts corporation (the "Company") and Investor Y (the "Stockholder").

Whereas, the Company has previously sold shares of its common stock ("Common Stock") to the Stockholder; and

Whereas, the Company is amending its Articles of Organization to remove certain provisions set forth therein which restrict the transfer of its Common Stock; and

Whereas, the parties desire to retain and impose certain restrictions on the shares of Common Stock presently owned by the Stockholders and on any new, additional or different shares of the capital stock of the Company which may at any time be issued to the Stockholder as a result of a recapitalization, stock dividend, split-up, combination or exchange of or on the Common Stock of the Company (collectively, all such Common Stock and any other such shares being referred to as "Shares");

Now, therefore, in consideration of the covenants and agreements set forth herein, and the mutual benefits which the parties anticipate from the performance thereof, the parties agree as follows.

1. Repurchase of Shares on Termination of Employment Relationship. Subject to the lapse provisions hereinafter set forth, if at any time the Stockholder's employment or consulting relationship with the Company is terminated for any reason whatsoever, including death or disability, the Company shall have the right (but not the obligation) to require the Stockholder to sell to the Company all or any part of the Shares at the cash price paid by the Stockholder therefor.

The Company's right of repurchase set forth in this Section 3 to purchase part or all of the Shares shall lapse as follows:

a. As to 100 percent of the Shares on February 1, 1990, if at least $180,000 in funding has not been received by the Company on or before such date.

b. If such funding has been received on or before such date, at the rate of 25 percent of such Shares each year for four years effective annually on the anniversary of this agreement.

The Company may exercise its right of repurchase of such Shares by giving written notice to the Stockholder or to his estate, personal representative or beneficiary ("Estate") at any time within 90 days of the termination of the Stockholder's employment with the Company, specifying the number of Shares to be sold to the Company. Such notice shall be effective only as to Shares as to which the Company's repurchase rights have not lapsed as of the date of such notice. Once such notice has been given, no further lapsing of such right of repurchase shall occur.

2. *Procedure for Sale of Shares.* In any notice given by the Company pursuant to Section 1 hereof, the Company shall specify a closing date for the repurchase transaction described herein. At the closing, the repurchase price shall be payable by the Company's check against receipt of certificates representing all Shares so repurchased. Upon the date of any such notice from the Company to the Stockholder or his Estate, the interest of the Stockholder in the Shares specified in the notice for repurchase shall automatically terminate, except for the Stockholder's right to receive payment from the Company for such Shares.

3. *Right of First Refusal.* If the Stockholder desires to sell all or any part of any Shares as to which the repurchase rights of the Company under Section 1 hereof have lapsed and an offeror (the "Offeror") has made an offer therefor, which offer the Stockholder desires to accept, the Stockholder shall: (i) obtain in writing an irrevocable and unconditional bona fide offer (the "Bona Fide Offer") for the purchase thereof from the Offeror; and (ii) give written notice (the "Option Notice") to the Company setting forth his desire to sell such Shares, which Option Notice shall be accompanied by a photocopy of the original executed Bona Fide Offer and shall set forth at least the name and address of the Offeror and the price and terms of the Bona Fide Offer. Upon receipt of the Option Notice, the Company shall have an option to purchase any or all of such

Shares specified in the Option Notice, such option to be exercisable by giving, within 30 days after receipt of the Option Notice, a written counternotice to the Stockholder. If the Company elects to purchase any or all of such Shares, it shall be obligated to purchase, and the Stockholder shall be obligated to sell to the Company, such Shares at the price and terms indicated in the Bona Fide Offer within 60 days from the date of receipt by the Company of the Option Notice.

The Stockholder may sell, pursuant to the terms of the Bona Fide Offer, any or all of such Shares not purchased by the Company for 30 days after expiration of the Option Notice, or for 30 days following a failure by the Company to purchase such Shares within 60 days of giving its counternotice of an intent to purchase such Shares; provided, however, that the Stockholder shall not sell such Shares to the Offeror if the Offeror is a competitor of the Company and the Company gives written notice to the Stockholder within 30 days of its receipt of the Option Notice stating that the Stockholder shall not sell his Shares to the Offeror; and provided, further, that prior to the sale of such Shares to the Offeror, the Offeror shall execute an agreement with the Company pursuant to which the Offeror agrees not to become a competitor of the Company and further agrees to be subject to the restrictions set forth in this Agreement. If any or all of such Shares are not sold pursuant to a Bona Fide Offer within the times permitted above, the unsold Shares shall remain subject to the terms of this Agreement.

The refusal rights of the Company set forth in Section 3 of this Agreement shall remain in effect until a distribution, if ever, to the public of shares of Common Stock for an aggregate public offering price of at least $3 million or more pursuant to a registration statement filed under the Securities Act of 1933, or a successor statute, at which time this Agreement will automatically expire.

Because the Shares cannot be readily purchased or sold in the open market, and for other reasons, the Stockholder and the Company acknowledge that the parties will be irreparably damaged in the event that this Agreement is not specifically enforced. Upon a breach or threatened breach of the terms, covenants and/or conditions of this Agreement by any of the parties hereto, the other party shall, in addition to all the other remedies, be entitled to a temporary or permanent injunction, without showing any actual damage, and/or a decree for specific performance, in accordance with the provisions hereof.

4. *Adjustments.* If there shall be any change in the Common Stock of the Company through merger, consolidation, reorganization, recapitalization, stock dividend, split-up, combination or exchange of shares, or the like, all of the terms and provisions of this Agreement shall apply to any new, additional or different shares or securities issued with respect to the Shares as a result of such event, and the repurchase price and the number of shares or other securities that may be repurchased under this Agreement shall be appropriately adjusted by the Board of Directors of the Company, whose determination shall be conclusive.

5. *Restrictions on Transfer.* The Stockholder agrees during the term of this Agreement that he will not sell, assign, transfer, pledge, hypothecate, mortgage or otherwise encumber or dispose of, by gift or otherwise (except to the Company), all or any of the Shares now or hereafter owned by him except as permitted by this Agreement.

The Company may place a legend on any stock certificate representing any of the Shares reflecting the restrictions on transfer and the Company's right of repurchase set forth herein and may make an appropriate notation on its stock records with respect to the same.

6. *Waiver of Restrictions.* The Company may at any time waive any restrictions imposed by any Section of this Agreement with respect to all or any portion of any of the Shares.

7. *No Obligation as to Employment.* The Company is not by reason of this Agreement obligated to start or continue the Stockholder in any employment or consulting capacity.

8. *Successors and Assigns.* This Agreement shall be binding on and inure to the benefit of the Company's successors and assigns and the Stockholder's transferees of the Shares, heirs, executors, administrators, legal representatives and assigns. Without limiting the foregoing, the Company is specifically permitted to assign its repurchase rights under Sections 1, 2 and 3 hereof.

9. *Notices.* All notices and other communications provided for or contemplated by this Agreement shall be delivered by hand or sent by certified mail, return receipt requested, addressed as follows:

If to the Company:

If to the Stockholder:

or to such address as the addressee may specify by written notice pursuant to this Section 10. Notices or communications sent by mail shall be deemed to have been given on the date of mailing. In the event of the Stockholder's death or incapacity, any notice or communication from the Company may, at the Company's option, be addressed either to the Stockholder at his last address specified pursuant to this Section 10 or to the Stockholder's Estate.

10. Governing Law. This Agreement shall be governed by and construed in accordance with the laws of the Commonwealth of Massachusetts.

11. Amendments; Waivers. Changes, amendments or modifications in or additions to or waivers of any provision under or of this Agreement may be made only by a written instrument executed by the parties hereto. Any waiver of any provision of this Agreement shall not excuse compliance with any other provision of this Agreement. Notwithstanding the foregoing, no course of dealing or delay on the part of either party in exercising any right shall operate as a waiver thereof or otherwise prejudice the rights of such holder.

The Stockholder acknowledges that the issuance of the Shares to the Stockholder hereunder satisfies and discharges in full any previous understanding between the Company and the Stockholder regarding the issuance of the Company's stock or option rights with respect thereto, and the Stockholder waives any preemptive rights he has to purchase any capital stock of the Company.

12. Captions. Captions are for convenience only and shall not be deemed to be part of this Agreement.

In witness whereof, the undersigned have caused this Agreement to be executed as an instrument under seal as of the day and year first above written.

Bibliography

GENERAL BACKGROUND AND REFERENCE

Frontiers of Entrepreneurship Research: 1981–1990, edited by J. A. Hornaday, J. A. Timmons, and K. H. Vesper et al., Babson College, Babson Park MA. These volumes include the complete proceedings of annual conferences on entrepreneurship research. The data-based papers cover every aspect of the venture creation process. The authors are from academia, government and the private sector, both in this country and abroad. These documents are the most comprehensive existing compendia of research into entrepreneurship.

Getting to Yes, Roger Fisher and William Ury, Houghton Mifflin, 1981. A useful book on the art of gaining agreement in a negotiation without giving in.

The New Venturers, John W. Wilson, Addison-Wesley, 1985. Good reading about the entrepreneurs and investors in some of America's most famous new companies of the past twenty years.

The Reality Bluebook, Vols I, II, Professional Publishing Company, San Rafael CA. The "bible" for real-estate entrepreneurs and brokers. Contains all the checklists, tables and tax considerations involved in buying or selling real estate, including how to do calculations on an HP 12C or HP 18C.

The Winning Performance: How America's High-Growth Midsize Companies Succeed, Donald K. Clifford, Jr., and Richard Cavanaugh, Bantam Books, 1985. Must reading for the growth-minded entrepreneur. The authors show evidence and examples of how and why new ventures "grow up big."

You Can Negotiate Anything, Herb Cohen, Bantam Books, 1980. A short but invaluable aid for anyone who has to negotiate anything. Don't leave home without it!

COMMERCIAL FINANCE

Financing the Growing Small Business, Thomas J. Martin, Holt, 1980. An excellent book on financing the small firm. Contains many practical examples, guidelines and suggestions. Includes a glossary, valuation guides and present value tables.

Small Business Guide to Borrowing Money, The, Richard L. Rubin and Philip Golberg, McGraw-Hill, 1980. Good discussion of how to work with different sources of capital. Includes sample forms and selected listings of venture capital firms and SBICs.

VENTURE CAPITAL

Financing and Investing in Private Companies, Arthur Lipper, III, Probus Publishing Co., 1988. A practical guide to financing private companies.

Financing and Managing Fast Growth Companies, G. Kozmetsky, M. D. Gill, Jr., and R. W. Smilor, Lexington Books, 1984. A useful book on the challenges of financing rapidly growing ventures.

Pratt's Guide to Venture Capital Sources, 12th ed., 1989, edited by Stanley Pratt. Articles written by experts on such subjects as business-plan preparation techniques, guidelines for working with venture capitalists, raising and using venture capital and going public. Also contains information on more than 700 venture capital companies and more than 60 small business underwriters.

Venture Capital Investing, William Gladstone, Prentice-Hall, 1988. A very practical and detailed book about the venture capital investing process from the investor's perspective. Specific lists of questions asked by venture capitalists as part of their screening and due diligence, for instance, provide a useful insight into how they go about their business.

Venture Economics, 75 Second Ave., Needham MA 02194. The information services, research and consulting division of Capital Publishing Corp., which publishes **Venture Capital Journal** and **Guide to Venture Capital Sources.** Venture Economics uses a proprietary database built up over the past 20 years to offer information on industry trends.

VIDEO TAPES

Beyond Start-Up, William Sahlman of Harvard Business School, Nathan/
Tyler, 1987, Boston. A behind-the-scenes look at five of America's
most successful founders, and an analysis of the stages of business
growth.

How to *Really* Start Your Own Business, *INC.* magazine, 1986. A lively
summary of the fundamental issues of new venture creation.

Shape of the Winner, The, Tom Peters, Video Publishing House, 1988.
A talk to 500 entrepreneurs attending a conference for high-growth
ventures in Boston in the fall of 1988.

NEWSPAPERS AND PERIODICALS

Timely, often provocative information for and about entrepreneurs
can be found in the following publications:

Babson Entrepreneurial Review, Babson College, Babson Park MA.
Organized and published by students at Babson College. Well
written, with timely, practical and informative articles for entrepreneurs.

Harvard Business Review—Growing Concerns (Soldiers Field Road,
Boston MA 02163).

Ideas (Ernst & Young Entrepreneurial Services Group, 2000 National
City Center, Cleveland OH 44114).

In Business (Box 323, Emmaus PA 18049).

INC. **Magazine** (38 Commercial Wharf, Boston MA 02110).

Journal of Business Venturing, Wharton Entrepreneurial Center, Phila-
delphia. A quarterly journal that focuses on new developments and
research.

Small Business Reporter (Bank of America, San Francisco CA).

Success Magazine (342 Madison Ave., New York NY 10173).

The New York Times frequently has items of interest to entrepreneurs.

The Wall Street Journal publishes a regular feature on small business.

Venture (35 W. 45th Street, New York NY 10036).

Index